D0876420

NO PLACE
TO BE
SOMEBODY

Look, man. You ain't let the slammers psyche you out? That ain't like you. That ain't like you at all.

NO PLACE TO BE SOMEBODY

A Black Black Comedy
in Three Acts

BY CHARLES GORDONE

Introduction by JOSEPH PAPP, Producer
New York Shakespeare Festival

The Bobbs-Merrill Company, Inc.
Indianapolis • New York

Note:
All rights, including professional, stock, amateur, motion picture, radio and television broadcasting, recitation and readings, are strictly reserved and no portion of these plays may be performed without written authorization. Inquiries about such rights may be addressed to the author's agent, Howard Rosenstone, William Morris Agency, 1350 Avenue of the Americas, New York, New York 10019

Photographs from the original production are by George E. Joseph

The Bobbs-Merrill Company, Inc.
A Subsidiary of Howard W. Sams & Co., Inc.
Publishers/Indianapolis • New York

To the memory of Sidney Bernstein, producer of ''The Blacks''

CAST

No Place To Be Somebody was first produced on May 2, 1969, at the New York Shakespeare Festival Public Theater, New York City, with the following cast in order of appearance:

Gabe Gabriel, *a young fairskinned Negro* . . . . Ron O'Neal
Shanty Mulligan, *a young white man* . . . . Ronnie Thompson
Johnny Williams, *a young Negro* . . . . Nathan George
Dee Jacobson, *a young white woman* . . . . Susan G. Pearson
Evie Ames, *a young Negro woman* . . . . Lynda Westcott
Cora Beasely, *a young Negro woman* . . . . Marge Eliot
Melvin Smeltz, *a young Negro man* . . . . Henry Baker
Mary Lou Bolton, *a white girl* . . . . Laurie Crews
Ellen, *a white girl* . . . . Iris Gemma
Sweets Crane, *an elderly Negro* . . . . Walter Jones
Mike Maffucci, *a young white man* . . . . Nick Lewis
Truck Driver, *a young white man* . . . . Michael Landrum
Judge Bolton, *a middle aged white man,*
        father of Mary Lou . . . . Ed Van Nuys
Machine Dog, *a young Negro (in*
        Johnny's imagination) . . . . Paul Benjamin
Sergeant Cappaletti, *a young white man* . . . . Charles Seals
Harry, *a Negro detective* . . . . Malcolm Hurd
Louie, *a young white man* . . . . Martin Shakar

The production was directed by Ted Cornell; sets and lighting were designed by Michael Davidson.

INTRODUCTION

It was with some trepidation that black playwright Charles Gordone handed the manuscript of his play NO PLACE TO BE SOMEBODY over to Ted Cornell, the very WASP director of the Public Experimental Theater, of the New York Shakespeare Festival. A more unlikely combination would be hard to find: Gordone, barefoot, bare-chested and pigtailed, looking more Iroquois-Chinese than African; Cornell, a blue-eyed, 24-year-old, shaggy-haired Yale Drama School student. Gordone must have thought, what could Cornell know about the black man's anger and what makes him laugh? And what about this Public Theater? True, it did produce HAIR and several other contemporary plays, but its main reputation was grounded in Shakespeare. All this seemed far from Gordone's idea of the right place for NO PLACE. But, Mr. Gordone was hungry and desperate, and after three years of trying to place his play, felt he could no longer afford too many quibbles.

A nervous agreement was concluded and the play went into rehearsal at THE OTHER STAGE, the experimental arm of the New York Shakespeare Festival Public Theater. All that was promised was three weeks of rehearsal and two weekends of performances for admission-free audiences. The playwright received $100.00. The work was projected as a kind of collaboration, which meant that the playwright would participate in the rehearsal process. It wasn't long before the director picked up the playwright's jargon, ducking and throwing "zingers," expressing approval with "that's out of sight." Gordone's suspicions began to dissolve as his respect for Cornell began to grow. This was a remarkable development, since the director was a relative new-comer to the theater, handling his first major assignment, while the author, as an experienced actor and director, was an old hand at the game. But they began to carry on a dialogue—direct, intense, often angry, never casual. Nobody was polite. The stage erupted with bursts of verbal violence, ghetto style, reflecting the strong feelings and emotions the play engendered among the black and white members of the cast.

The transition from the text to rehearsal to performance was almost indiscernible. There was a continuous flow of life from the outside that crossed the threshold of the theater with no apparent conflict. Visiting rehearsals, I was hard put to distinguish the play from the heated arguments over its interpretation. Both were a part of the same fantastic reality.

The crucial test of any play's validity comes when it confronts its first audience. The Experimental Theater has a seating capacity of 109 and was filled to overflowing when NO PLACE opened with an audience mixed almost equally black and white. Although the surface of NO PLACE TO BE SOMEBODY suggests black militant melodrama—exciting, funny, violent—its very complexities and ambiguities provided no clear-cut feelings of satisfaction for either black or white members of the audience. What it did achieve was a rich confrontation of the black man and himself, the white man and himself, and then placed those selves face to face with each other.

This exciting fusion which is the magic that makes good theater takes place at every performance of the play. It is testimony to the gifts of an important new playwright, and the talent and energy of the company as a whole. The initial audience reaction brought in the critics. As a result, NO PLACE TO BE SOMEBODY is now a hit and has moved to a larger theater within the Public Theater complex. However, its genesis in production in a free experimental theater also says something as to where we may reasonably look for renewal of the theater in America.

Joseph Papp

New York, July 1969

They ain't no law. They kill you and me in the name of the law!

NO PLACE TO BE SOMEBODY

ACT ONE

SCENE ONE

Time: The past fifteen years
Place: New York City
Setting: Johnny's Bar
At rise: GABE sits near jukebox, typing. Rips page from
typewriter. Balls it up, flings it angrily at audience.

Gabe

Excuse me. Forgot you were out there. My name is Gabe. Gabe Gabriel, to be exact. I'm a writer. Didn't mean to lose my temper. Something I've been working on all my life. Not losing my temper.

> *Takes out marihuana cigarette. Lights it. Inhales it. Holds*
> *smoke in.*

Right now I'm working on a play. They say if you wanna be a writer you gotta go out an' live. I don't believe that no more. Take my play for instance. Might not believe it but I'm gonna make it all up in my head as I go along. Before I prove it to you, wanna warn you not to be thinkin' I'm tellin' you a bunch'a barefaced lies. An' no matter how far out I git, don't want you goin' out'a here with the idea what you see happenin' is all a figment of my grassy imagination. 'Cause it ain't!

> *He picks up Bible from table. Raises it above his head.*
> *Without looking turns pages.*

"And I heard a Voice between the banks of the U'Lai. And it called, Gabriel! Gabriel! Make this man understand the vision! So He came near where I stood! And when He came, I was frightened and fell upon my face!"

3

He closes Bible. As he exits, lights dim out, then come up on SHANTY, at jukebox. Jazz is playing. SHANTY takes out his drumsticks. Begins to rap on bar. JOHNNY enters. Hangs up raincoat and umbrella.

Johnny
Cool it, Shanty.

Shanty
Man, I'm practicing.

Johnny
Damned if that bar's anyplace for it. Git on that floor there.

Shanty
Puts drumsticks away. Takes broom.
Ever tell you 'bout the time I went to this jam session? Max Roach was there. Lemme sit in for him.

Johnny
Said you played jus' like a spade.

Shanty
What's wrong with that? Ol' Red Taylor said wasn't nobody could hold a beat an' steady cook it like me. Said I had "the thing"! Member one time we played "Saints." For three hours, we played it.

Johnny
Had to git a bucket'a col' water an' throw it on you to git you to quit, huh?

Shanty
One these days I'm gonna have me a boss set'a skins for my comeback. Me an' Cora was diggin' a set up on "Four-Six Street." Sump'm else ag'in. Bass drum, dis'pearin' spurs, snares, tom-toms. . . .

Johnny
Gon' steal 'em?

Shanty
I been savin' up. Gonna git me them drums. Know what I'm gonna do then? I'm gonna quit you flat. Go for that. Sheee! I ain't no lifetime apron. That's for damned sure.

Johnny
Yeah, well meantime how 'bout finishin' up on that floor? Time to open the store.
DEE and EVIE enter. Hang coats up.
You broads let them two ripe apples git away from you, huh?

Dee
Don't look at me.

4

Evie

Aw, later for you an' your rich Texas trade.

Dee

Just gettin' too damned sensitive.

Evie

Sensitive my black behin'! Excuse me, I mean black ass.
Goes to jukebox. Punches up number.

Dee

Last night we bring those two johns up to her pad. An' like, Jack? One with the cowboy hat? Stoned? Like out of his skull. And like out of no-where he starts cryin'.

Evie

All weekend it was "Nigger this an' Nigger that."

Dee

Never bothered you before. I didn't like it when he started sayin' things like "The black sons a'bitches are gettin' to be untouchables! Takin' over the country!"

Evie

Bet he'll think twice before he says sump'm like that ag'in.

Dee

That lamp I gave her? One the senator brought me back from Russia? Evie goes an' breaks it over his head.

Johnny

What the hell'd you do that for?

Evie

Sure hated to lose that lamp.

Johnny

Wouldn't care if they b'longed to the Ku Klux Klan long's they gimme the bread.
He goes into DEE's purse.

Shanty

Sure had plenty of it too! When they was in here, they kept buyin' me drinks. Thought I was the boss.

Johnny

Crackers cain't 'magine Niggers runnin' nothin' but elevators an' toilets.

Dee

Leave me somethin', please.

Evie

5 Ain't gon' do nothin' with it nohow.

Johnny
> *Finds pair of baby shoes in* DEE's *purse.*

Thought I tole you to git rid'a these?

Dee

I forgot.

Johnny

Save you the trouble.
> *He starts to throw them away.*

Dee

Don't you do that, you black bastard. So help me, Johnny.

Evie

Aw, let 'er have them things, Nigger! Wha's the big deal?

Johnny

'Tend to your own business, bitch. Ain't a minute off your ass for messin' it up las' night.

Evie

Excuse me. Didn't know you was starvin' to death.

Johnny
> *Goes for* EVIE *but quickly checks himself when she reaches for her purse. He turns back to* DEE.

Look'a here, girl. I ain't gon' have no harness bulls knockin' down yo' door.

Dee

All of a sudden you worried about me.

Johnny

Jus' git rid'a that crap. Worrin' over sump'm pass, over an' done with.
> CORA *enters. A wet newspaper covers her head.*

Cora

Lawd'a mercy! Now I gotta do this un'form all over ag'in. Bad as I hate to iron.

Johnny

Ironin' for them crackers. Cain't see why you cain't iron for yourself.

Cora

This ain't no maid's un'form as any fool kin see. I makes my livin' as a pract'cal nurse. I ain't nobody's maid.

Johnny

Somebody tole me they seen you wheelin' a snotty nose, blue-eyed baby th'ough Washin'ton Square the other day.

Cora

They was a Wash'ton Square lie. Onlies' baby I wheel aroun' gon' be my own.

6

Johnny

Hell! By the time you an' Shanty git aroun' to somethin' like that . . . you ain't gon' wheel nothin' roun' but a tray'a black-ass coffee.

> DEE and EVIE *laugh.*

Cora

You cheap husslers don't hit the street, you gon' be sellin' yo' wares in'a home for the cripple an' infirm.

Evie

Gon' have to bring ass to git ass.

> CORA *comes off her stool. Jerks off shoe.* EVIE *comes up with a switchblade.*

Johnny

Hey! Hey! Git under the bed with that shit!

> *He races around bar. Comes between them.*

What the hell's the matter with you, Cora? Cain't you take a little joke?

Cora

Don't know why every time I come in here, I gotta be insulted by you an' these here Harlows.

> EVIE *still has her knife out.*

Evie

Bet if that heifer messes with me, I'll carve her up like'a fat piece'a barbecue.

Johnny

Naw you won't neither. Not in here, you won't. Put it away! I said put it away.

> EVIE *reluctantly puts knife away.*

Dee

Let's get out of here, Evie. She's always pickin' her nose about somethin'.

Evie

She don't scare me none. Jus' smells bad, tha's all.

Dee

> *Looks at her watch.*

Well, I gotta date, and you gotta see your headshrinker, don't you?

Johnny

Headshrinker? Damned if Evie ain't gone an' got herself a pimp.

Evie

He don't come as expensive as some pimps I know.

Dee

> *Goes for the coats.*

7   Now, don't you two start up again.

The two women start for the street doors.

Johnny
Make money, baby. Make that money.

Dee
That's all you ever think about. Can't you just dig me for my soul?

Johnny
Wrong color be talkin' 'bout soul.

Dee
Negroes. Think you gotta corner on soul.

Evie
Us has suffahd, das why.

        DEE *and* EVIE *exit.*

Cora
Gimme a martini, Shangy. Gotta bad taste in my mouth.

Johnny
Make sure she pays for that drink.

Cora
I works an' I pays. I don't ask a livin' ass for nothin'.

Johnny
'Member when you did.

Cora
I was broke. Couldn't fin' no work. 'Sides I had you to take care of! Like I p'omised yo' mama I would. 'Fore she died. Till you had to go git in trouble with that Eye-tralian boy.

Johnny
Maybe I jus' got tired'a all them col'-cuts an' fuck-ups.

Cora
When you got out'a that 'form school, I was ready to take care you ag'in! But that bad Nigger Sweets Crane got holt you an' ruint ya.

Johnny
Fixed it so's I didn't have to go to that orphan-house, didn't he? Took me in, treated me like I was his own son, didn't he? Damned sight more'n you or that drunken bitch of a mama'a mine did.

Cora
Jay Cee? Might God strike you dead. Maybe I ain't yo' flesh an' blood. But yo' mama? She couldn't he'p none'a the things she did.

Johnny
Do me one favor, bitch. Leave my mama on the outside. 'Nother thing, if you cain't say nothin' boss 'bout Sweets Crane, you don't have to come in here yo' dam-self.

8

He slaps her on the behind and exits to the kitchen.

Cora

Well, fan me with a brick! Tha's one Nigro you jus' cain't be civil with.

She sips her drink as SHANTY *finishes sweeping floor.*

Eb'm as a chile—give him a piece'a candy, wudn't the kin' he wanted, he'd rare back an' th'ow it at you. An' he'd stan' there lookin' all slang-eyed darin' you to touch him.

She watches SHANTY *beat on the bar.*

Never had no papa. 'Less you call that ol' dog Sweets Crane a father. His mama was always sickly an' she did drink. Never would give it out though, who it was did it to her. Carried that to her grave!

She downs her drink.

I knowed her ever since I was a li'l gal down South. You know, they was always sump'm funny 'bout her. Swore Jay Cee was born with a veil over his face.

Shanty

A what?

Cora

A veil over his face. Ev'body knows babies born with veils over they faces is s'pose to see ghostes an' raise forty-one kin's'a hell.

Shanty

Johnny? Sheee.

Cora

If I'm lyin', I'm flyin'!

Shanty

Cora, you're superstishus as hell.

Cora

Cain't he'p but be, li'l bit. My peoples all had fogey-isms. Where I come from ev'body had 'em. One kin' or 'nother.

> MELVIN *enters, hangs up knapsack and rain jacket, takes cap off. Knocks the wet from his pants. His head is almost clean-shaven.*

Chile! you sho' don't have to worry 'bout yo' head goin' back home!

Melvin

My home, sweety, is in Saint Albans. You don't have to inform me as to where yours is.

He goes into a soft-shoe dance and sings.

"Where the people beat they feet on the Mississippi mud."

Cora

Now, ain't that jus' like you ig'orint Nigroes. If they cain't think'a nothin' to say, they start slippin' you into the dozens.

Johnny
> *Enters from kitchen.*

You late, Mel.

Melvin

Today was my dance class, remember? Anyway, who can get a cab in this weather?

Johnny

White folks, baby. Wheeeet folks!

Melvin

Objectively speaking, plenty of them were passed up too.
> *He begins to stretch his leg muscles.*

Johnny

Dig? One these days we gon' see this on tee vee.

Melvin

You got your people mixed. The dances they do on television is ster-ictly commercial.

Johnny

What hell's wrong with that? If you gon' run 'roun' wigglin' yo' tukus, mights well git paid for it.

Melvin

I study with a great artist! He deplores that sort of thing.

Johnny

Whozis great artist you study with?

Melvin

Victor Weiner! He teaches the Chenier method.

Johnny

This Shimmy-yay method you don't wiggle the tukus?

Melvin

Why?

Johnny

Them turkeys on tee vee mus' make a whole lotta coins jus' for wigglin' they tukeruseys.

Melvin

Prostitutes. All of them.

Johnny

Pros'tutes, huh?
> *He goes to jukebox. Punches up number. Classical music comes on.*

Go with a little sample what you jokers is puttin' down.

Melvin
Nothing doing. To appreciate true art, one must first be familiar with it.

Cora
Talk that talk, Mel. What do Jay Cee know 'bout bein' artistic?

Johnny
Rejects the music.
This Wineberg you study with? He's a Jew, ain't he?

Melvin
So what?

Johnny
Gotta give it to him. Connin' spades into thinkin' they gotta be taught how to dance.

Melvin
You're just prejudiced, Johnny. That's why you have no appreciation.

Johnny
When you start teachin' him, maybe I'll git me some pre-she-a-shun.
A loud voice is heard offstage.

Voice
Inn keeper!

Gabe
Bursts in clad in army raincoat and Sou'wester. He brandishes an umbrella and briefcase.
Cock-a-doodle-doo!
JOHNNY paws the floor with his feet.
"I am a ringtailed squeeler. I am that very infant that refused his milk before his eyes was opened an' called out for a bottle of old rye."
They circle each other.

Johnny
"This is me! Johnny Earthquake. I rassle with light'nin', put a cap on thunder. Set every mammy-jammer in the graveyard on a wonder."

Gabe
"I grapple with lions! Put knots in they tails! Sleep on broken glass an' for breakfast, eat nails. I'm a ba-a-a-d mother-for-ya."
JOHNNY goes behind the bar and takes down a bottle of whisky as GABE spies CORA.
Eeeeeow! I feel like swallowin' a nappy-headed woman whole!

Cora
Pushes him away playfully.
11 Better stay out'a my face, fool.

JOHNNY *moves around bar to center. Theatrically pours a waterglass half-full of whisky. Sets glass before GABE on table. GABE removes coat and hat. Hands them to CORA. He eyes the whisky. Sniffs. Picks up the glass.*

A-Lawd! Gabe you ain't. . . .

GABE *puts the glass to his lips and begins to drink.*

Ooooo!

GABE *is emptying the glass.*

Ooooo!

He finishes. Eyes crossed. Sets the glass down. Grimaces. Shakes his head. JOHNNY and SHANTY laugh.

I swear! Y'all is sho' crazy. Ain't neither one'a ya got good sense.

Gabe
Needed that. Needed that one bad. Gimme another one.

SHANTY *reaches for the bottle.*

Cora
Don't you do it, Shangy. Let that fool kill hisse'f. Ain't no call for you to he'p him.

Johnny
Dam, Gabe! You ain't done gone an' got alcoholic on us?

Gabe
Don't you worry yo' li'l happy head 'bout me, sir. Matter fact, I'm cuttin' myself right out'a the herd.

Johnny
Tell me sump'm, baby? Is this herd pink? An' got snoots an' grea' big ears?

Gabe
No they ain't. In color, they're black with big, thick, lip-pussys.

Johnny
Man! Them ain't elephants you been hangin' out with, them's hippo-bottom'a-the-pot'a-muses!

JOHNNY *and GABE give each other some skin.*

Cora
Lawd! What in the devil an' Tom Walker you Nigros talkin' 'bout now?

Johnny
Keep her in the dark, Gabe. Keep that mulyan in the black.

Melvin
They're talking about Gabe's audition, Cora. Gabe had an audition today.

12

Gabe

I said it was a herd call, Melvino Rex!

Melvin

Lots of actors there, huh?

Gabe

Actors? Actors did you say? Well, yes! Every damned black actor in town.

Cora

Well, why didn't you say so in the first place? Lawd, chile! You ought'a lean up off this stuff.

> GABE *tries to put his arm around her.*

An' take yo' arm out from 'roun' my neck.

Melvin

How'd you make out at that audition, Gabe?

Gabe

Dig this. It was a musical! A musical about slavery.

Melvin

Slavery? Well! It's about time.

Johnny

Gabe's gon' play'a ha'f-white house Nigger! An' they ain't no whiter, ha'f-white house Nigger in New Yawk than Gabe is, I'll bet'a fat man.

Gabe

You jus'a-got-dat-wrong, John. Stage manager calls me over. Whispers they're auditionin' the white actors tomorrow. Baby! I refuse to see anything musical at all about slavery.

> *Everyone breaks up laughing.*

Cora

Say, Gabe? How about doin' one o' them crazy po'ms'a your'n? Ain't heard none in a long time.

Shanty

Yeah, Gabe! How 'bout it?

Melvin

Might make you feel better.

Johnny

Git under the bed with that shit! Ain't runnin' no cabaret. Fixin' to git me a summons!

Gabe

What you wanna hear?

Cora

13 Anythin'.

Johnny

If you jus' gotta. Knowin' you, you always jus' gotta. Make it sump'm you know.

Gabe

Dig this one.

> *All except JOHNNY eagerly take seats.*

They met on the banks of the Potomac, the rich, the great and the
   small!
It's impossible to tell you, should'a been there an' seen it all!
They came by train, by plane, by bus an' by car!
Bicycle an' tricycle from near an' very far!
On mule an' on horseback!
With greasy bag an' kroker sack!
Buckboard an' clapboard an' goats pullin' wagons!
Tin lizzies an' buggies an' trucks so weighted down with people, you
   could see the backends saggin'!
Carts with motors, an' trams!
Wheelchairs an' wheelbarrels an' women pushin' prams!
Little boys on scooters! Little girls on skates!
Beatnicks, hippies an' hoboes, most of them had come by freights!
We had walked in light-footed an' barefooted, had walked all out'a
   our shoes! Some hopped it on crutches for days!
An' then we got the news, some black power agitators was arrested
   along the way!
'Course they was a lotta Cadillacs an' Buicks, rich people showin' off!
   I didn't pay that no min',
I jus' took comfort in the thought we needed people of every kin'!
An' if all America had been there or seen it on tee vee,
They would'a knowed we all meant business in gittin' our e-kwa-le-
   tee!
Well, we moved to the square with the pool in the middle!
While we waited, some strange young folk from New Yawk played a
   flute an' a fiddle!
Then somebody pro-nounced that reb'm somebody would pray!
An' by the settin' sun, we knelt in the dust'a that day!
Somebody else got up with a great loud voice!
Said they had on han' the speaker of our choice!
Said this black man was a black man of black deeds an' black fame!
(I'll be damned to hell, I disremember his name!)
Then a hush fell on all them people that night,
'Cause we was there for one thing, our civil right!   14

This black man, he rizzed up an' walked to the stan'! I could tell at a
  glance that he was the man!
An' he boomed out over that mickey-phone an' called for all black
  folk to unite an' not roam to other orguzashuns who jus' wanted to
  fight white people an' git what they can in a country that would
  soon give liberty an' 'quality to every man!
If we worked long an' hard, he admitted it'd be rough!
But he said, black unity an' solidarity would be enough!
Then he rizzed up his arms an' bobbled his head!
Best as I kin I'll try to remember what he said!
        GABE *pretends he is skinning a team of mules.*
Hya!
You, Afro-Americans!
Hya!
You, American Afros!
Hya!
You Muslims an' nay-cee-pees!
Hya!
You so-called Negroes!
Tan liberals!
Black radicals!
Hya!
You respec-rabble black boorwahzeees!
Hya!
Black Demos an' 'Publicans,
Git back on the track!
You Nash-na-lissys and Marx-a-sissies
Who all been pin-pointin' black!
Hya!
You half-white pro-fesh-nals!
Hya!
Civil rights pro-sesh-nals!
Hya!
You cursed sons-a-ham!
Don't rock no boat!
Don't cut ne'r th'oat!
Be a beacon for some black magazeen!
Come doctor!
Come lawyer!
Come teacher!
Black employer!
An' keepers of white latrines!
On Donner!

On Blitzen!
You black nick-surd-rich-ins!
On! On! With the soul kweezeen!
You inter-urbans!
Satisfied suburbans!
To you, I gotta say whoa!
What's needed to save us
Is not Some-a-Davus!
Or even Benjammer O.!
Giddy-up! Yippeee-ay! Or Kidney Poteeay!
They already got they dough!
Now, here are the bare facks,
Grab yo' selves by the bootblacks!
Leave Heroin Manderson on the side!
An' all you take notice,
You'll all git yo' lettuce!
You'll own the post office yet!
Off-springs off mixed couples
Who're more than a han'fu,
You'll make the cover of Jet!
We'll have invented a machine that delivers
A cream to make crackers pay the debt!
Now junkies don't dilly
You husslers don't dally!
Don't waste yo' time smokin' pot
In some park or some alley,
'Cause Cholly is watchin' you!"

Well, he would a'went that'a way
To this very day but his th'oat
It got too hoarse!
When he sat down wasn't a clap ner a soun',
Couldn't tell if he'd got to the end!
A cracker preacher there, then said a prayer!
Said civil rights you could not fo'ce!
By this time I was so confused my head was in a spin!
Somebody else got up with a grinnin' face!
Said to leave that place like we found it!
Tha's when I reached in my pocket an' pulled out my packet an' be-
    fore everybody took a sip'a my wine!
Then we lef' that place without ne'r trace!
An' we didn't leave ne'r chit'lin' behin'!
            Everyone laughs and claps his hands.   16

Johnny

If you ask me, it's all a big-ass waste'a time an' energy. Jus' how long you gon' keep this up? Ought'a be in some office makin'a white man's pay.

Gabe

Sheee! Think I'd rather be hawkin' neckbones on a Hundred an' Twenty-Fifth Street.

Cora

Uh-aw! Better git out'a here 'fore you two start goin' at it agin.
> She gets newspaper and peers out of window.

An' 'fore it starts up rainin' ag'in! Lawd knows I ain't prepared for neither one.
> She moves to MELVIN who is stirring something in a skillet. She sniffs.

Shanty! If you want sump'm 'sides Mel's warmed-over chili better see you for supper.

Gabe

Better watch it, Shanty. She's thinkin' the way to a man's heart is through his stomach.

Cora

> Moves to street doors.

Sho' ain't no way to stay there.
> She exits. MELVIN exits to kitchen. SHANTY busies himself. GABE sits. Looks thoughtful. JOHNNY tosses him some bills.

Gabe

What's this?

Johnny

Aw, take the bread, nigger.
> GABE does not pick up the money.

Look'a here, Gabe. I know you think I'm all up 'side the wall. You hip to the books an' all like'a that. But ser-us-ly! Why ain't they doin' you no good?

Gabe

Let's jus' say I ain't in no big rush.

Johnny

It's Charlie, ain't it?

Gabe

What about Charlie?

Johnny

It's wrote all over you! Might be foolin' some people. Cock-a-doodle-dooin' an' comin' on with yo' funky po'try. . . .

Gabe

When you git me some answers other than the one's you been handin' me, I'll git in the bed with you.

Johnny

One thing Sweets says to me, 'fore he got his time. He says. . . .

Gabe

Screw it, John. When you start bringin' Sweets into the picture, I know exactly what's comin' next. The answer is still negative.

Johnny

Still wanna believe you kin sell papers an' become President, huh? Snowballs in Egypt.

Gabe

I ain't lookin' to break no law.

Johnny

They ain't no law. They kill you an' me in the name'a the law. You an' me wouldn't be where we at, if it wasn't for the law. Even the laws they write for us makes us worse off.

Gabe

From the git-go, they don't operate like Sweets anymore. Harlem's all caught up.

Johnny

Who's operatin' in Harlem?

Gabe

You cain't be thinkin' about down here! It was branchin' out'a Harlem got Sweets where he's at right now.

Johnny

Man, what you think I been doin' the ten years Sweets been in the joint? I tell you the scheme is together. Me an' him gon' git us a piece'a this town.

Gabe

An' end up on the bottom'a the East River with it tied aroun' your necks.

Johnny

Bet we'll have us a box'a crackers under each armpit if we do!

Gabe

Well, I don't dig crackers that much.

18

Johnny
Okay, Hollywood! Keep knockin' on doors with yo' jeans at half-mast. Sellin' yo'self like some cheap-ass whore. If I know one thing about you, you ain't that good'a actor. Whitey knows right away you cain't even stan' to look at him.
GABE *grins, picks money up. Pockets it. Blackout.*

SCENE TWO

Time: A week later
Place: The same
Setting: The same
At rise: GABE stands at center.

Gabe
When I'm by myself like this, for days, weeks, even months at a
time, it sort'a gets to me! I mean deep down inside things begin to
happen. Lemme confess, sometimes I git to feelin'—like I get so
vicious, I wanna go out an' commit mass murder. But don't mis-
understand me. Because I call myself a black playwright, don't git
the impression I'm hung up on crap like persecution an' hatred.
'Cause I ain't! I'm gonna leave that violence jazz to them cats who are
better at it than me. I ain't been out of the house in over two
months. Not because I been that busy, I just been too damned
scared. I been imaginin' all kind'a things happenin' out there. An'
they're waitin' just for me. All manner of treachery an' harm. But
don't think because of it my play is about Negro self-pity. Or even
that ol' "You-owe-me-whitey party line." 'Cause it ain't. In spite of
what I learned in college, it did not give me that introduction to suc-
cess, equality an' wealth, that to my parents were the most logical al-
ternatives to heaven. Anyway, like I say, I'm gonna leave that social
protest jive to them cats who are better equipped than me.
　　　　Lights dim out on GABE and come up on JOHNNY, who
　　　　is asleep on the floor. One shoe is off and an empty bot-

tle and glass lie nearby. A telegram is pushed under the door. JOHNNY rouses himself. Puts on his shoe and goes to the door. Picks up the telegram and studies it. Someone is heard trying the street doors. He hides the telegram and opens the door. DEE enters. Goes behind the bar. Makes a Bromo. JOHNNY takes out the telegram. Peers at it again.

Dee
What is it?

Johnny
Looks like a telegram from Sweets.
>*He gives her the telegram.*

Read it.
>*DEE downs her Bromo.*

Read it, I said.
>*She picks up the telegram.*

Dee
It's from Sweets allright.

Johnny
Well, what does it say?

Dee
Says he's going to be released in three weeks.
>*JOHNNY snatches telegram.*

Makes you pretty happy, doesn't it?

Johnny
Babeee! Happy ain't the word! I am dee-ler-russ! Yeeeeoweee!

Dee
>*Grabs her head.*

Hold it down, will ya?

Johnny
S'matter? Rough night?

Dee
What else?

Johnny
Go home! Cop some zees!

Dee
Just sit here for a while! If you don't mind.

Johnny
Dam'dest thing. Las' night I stayed here. Burnt one on. Fell asleep   22

right here. Had this dream. 'Bout Sweets gittin' out. Man, tha's weird! Tha's damned weird.

Dee
Today's my birthday.

Johnny
Dam! Forgot all about it.

Dee
Wish to hell I could.

Johnny
Anybody'd think you was a wrinkled up ol' mulyan.
> *He takes money from her purse. Tosses her a few bills, stuffs the rest into his pocket.*

Here. Go out an' buy yourself sump'm real nice.

Dee
> *Flinging the bills back at him.*

I don't want anything for my birthday.

Johnny
Now, lissen. Don't you start no shit this mornin'. I'm in too good'a humor.

Dee
Johnny. Let's you and me just take off for somewhere! For a couple of weeks.

Johnny
You off your wood, girl? With Sweets gittin' out?

Dee
I gotta bad feelin'

Johnny
I don't give'a dam what kind'a feelin' you got. Sweets was like a father to me.

Dee
So you told me. A thousand times you told me.

Johnny
I know. That bitch Evie's been puttin' ideas into your head.

Dee
That's not true. You lay off her, Johnny.

Johnny
Lissen to her, she'll have you husslin' tables at Howard Johnson's.

Dee
23 Might be better off.

Johnny

> *Slaps her.*

Kiss me an' tell me you sorry.

Dee

> *She kisses him.*

Sorry.

> *She moves to street doors.*

Johnny

Hey, girl. Gotta celebrate your birthday some way. Tomorrow mornin'. Bring over the Sunday papers an' a bottle'a my bes' wampole. "All day, all night, Mary Ann!"

> DEE *exits.* JOHNNY *peers at telegram. Goes to jukebox. Punches up number. Presently* CORA *and* SHANTY *enter.*

Cora

Jay Cee? I know it ain't none'a my business, but that woman'a yours? She's out there in the car. Jus'a cryin' her eyeballs out.

Johnny

> *Getting his jacket, moving to street doors.*

Hol' down the store, Shanty. Be back in'a couple'a hours.

> *He exits.* SHANTY *goes to door. Locks it. Punches up number on jukebox.*

Cora

Shangy? I been doin' some thinkin'. You heard anything from Gloria?

Shanty

Heard what?

Cora

'Bout yo' divorce! Tha's what.

Shanty

Gloria ain't gonna give me no die-vo'ce.

Cora

Well, if she ain't that don't stop us from livin' together, do it?

Shanty

What made you change your mind?

Cora

'Nother thing. Ever since I knowed you, you been belly-achin' 'bout gittin' you some drums.

Shanty

Gonna git 'em too!

Cora

Well, I'm willin' to do everything I kin to help you.

Shanty

You mean—you mean, you'd help me git 'em? No jive?

Cora

Then you could quit ol' Jay Cee an' go back to playin' in them night-clubs like you said you used to.

Shanty

You really mean it? You'd help me git my drums?

Cora

Ain't talkin' jus' to hear myse'f rattle.

Shanty

Mama, you are the greatest.

> *He hugs her.*

Cora

Honey, hush.

Shanty

Know what I'm gonna do, Cora? Soon's I git them drums I'm gonna bring 'em in here. Set 'em up an' play "the thing" for Johnny.

Cora

Lawd, Shangy! I wouldn't miss that for nothin' in this worl'.

> SHANTY *takes out marihuana cigarette. Wets, lights it. Smokes.*

Lawd, Shangy! I done tole you 'bout smokin' them ol' nasty things.

> *He passes the cigarette to her. She grins.*

Guess it won't hurt none once in a while.

> *She inhales. Coughs.*

Shanty

I was just thinkin' about ol' Gloria. How much she hated jazz. Nigger music, she called it. Man, every time I'd set up my skins to practice, she'd take the kids an' go over to her mother's.

> *They begin to pass the cigarette back and forth.*

Dig? One night after a gig, brought some cats over for a little game. Some spade cat grabs her between the legs when I wasn't lookin'.

Cora

Spent the bes' part'a my life on Nigros that won't no good. Had to baby an' take care all of 'em.

Shanty

Never heard the last of it. You'd think he raped her or somethin'.

Cora

Cain't hol' no job! Take yo' money an' spen' it all on likker.

Shanty
Got this job playin' the Borsh-Belt. My skins was shot! Had to borrow a set from Champ Jones.

Cora
Cain't make up their min's! Jus' be a man, I says.

Shanty
Gone about a week. Come home. Shades all down. Key won't fit in the door.

Cora
Git evil. Nex' thing you know they goin' up 'side yo' head.

Shanty
She's over at her mother's. Says she gonna sue me for desershun.

Cora
I thought you was a dif'rent kind'a Nigger. I'm gon' git me a white man, one that'll take care me. Or he'p me take care myse'f.

Shanty
I never did nothin' to her.

Cora
Tha's when he went up 'side my head with the ash tray!

Shanty
Said she needed some bread. Went to the bank. Cashed my check. Come back. Skins the cat loaned me are gone.

Cora
I loved him so much.

Shanty
Grabbed a broom out'a the closet. Went to work on the bitch.

Cora
Them awful things he said to me.

Shanty
Bitch never made a soun' or dropped a tear.

Cora
I cried sump'm ter'ble.

Shanty
Says I'd never see my kids ag'in or the drums neither.

Cora
Wanted children so bad! Doctor said I couldn't have none.

Shanty
Started chokin' her. Would'a killed her, if my kid hadn't jumped on my back.

26

Cora

Ain't hard to satisfy me. 'Cause Lawd knows I ain't never asked for much.

Shanty

One thing I learned. Stay away from bitches like that. Just ain't got no soul.

> *He gets can of spray deodorant. Opens street doors and sprays the bar.*

Cora

> *Rouses herself. Wipes tears.*

Shangy! I sho' wanna see Jay Cee's face when he sees you play them drums.

> *Blackout.*

SCENE THREE

Time: Three weeks later
Place: The same
Setting. The same
At rise: MELVIN is doing his dance exercises. JOHNNY enters with white tablecloth and slip of paper. SHANTY busies himself behind the bar.

Johnny
Sure we need all this, Mel?

Melvin
You hired me to be a short order cook around here. That's exactly what that list is too. A short order.

Johnny
Jus' checkin'. Don't want you slippin' none'a that what-wuzzit over on me ag'in.

Melvin
Po-tahge par-mun-teeay. Everybody else liked it.

Johnny
Been some chit'lin's, you'da been sayin' sump'm.

Melvin
Chit'lin's? Sometimes I think you have the taste-buds of a slave.
> *He snatches the slip of paper out of JOHNNY's hands and exits as MARY LOU BOLTON enters and goes to a table.*

Johnny
Sump'm I kin do for you?

Mary Lou
I'd like a daiquiri, please. . . .

Johnny
Got any identification?

Mary Lou
Really!

Johnny
Mary Lou Bo—

Mary Lou
Mary Lou Bolton.

Johnny
This the school you go to?

Mary Lou
Just graduated.

Johnny
>*Goes behind the bar to mix drink.*

Buddy'a mine come out'a there. . . .

Mary Lou
Elmira is an all-woman's school.

Johnny
I mean the slammers up there.

Mary Lou
Beg your pardon?

Johnny
>*Sets drink before her.*

Prison.

Mary Lou
Oh, yes! My father spent a lot of time up there.

Johnny
You kiddin'? Your father did?

Mary Lou
>*She laughs.*

He was a criminal lawyer.

Johnny
He ain't no lawyer no more?

Mary Lou
He's a judge now.

Johnny
Must'a been a hell of a lawyer.

Mary Lou
Oh, I suppose so. . . .

Johnny
What you mean, you s'pose so?

Mary Lou
I'd rather not discuss it.

Johnny
Sorry.

> ELLEN *enters. Carries a civil rights placard.*

Ellen
C'mon, Mary! Everyone's waitin' on you.

Mary Lou
Be there in a second, Ellen.

> *She looks into her purse.* ELLEN *exits.*

What do I owe you for the drink?

Johnny
Ain't you gonna finish it?

Mary Lou
I really shouldn't. But this is my first time out! Kind of nervous, you know?

Johnny
First time out?

Mary Lou
We're picketing the construction work up the street. The new hospital they're building.

Johnny
What for?

Mary Lou
Haven't you heard? The unions won't accept qualified Negroes.

Johnny
Why don't them qualified Nigroes do they own pickitin'?

Mary Lou
It's everyone's responsibility.

Johnny
You only git in the way.

Mary Lou
I'm glad all Negroes don't feel the way you do.

Johnny
You don't know how I feel.

Mary Lou
> *Puts a bill on the table and prepares to leave.*

I don't think I care to find out.

Johnny
Jus' happen to think somebody invented this civil rights jive to git a whole lotta people runnin' in the wrong direction.

Mary Lou
> *Starts to move to street doors. JOHNNY catches her by the arm.*

Would you mind?

Johnny
Know what's in that daiquiri, baby?

Mary Lou
Let me go, please.

Johnny
Jizzum juice. A triple dose of jizmistic juice. Any minute you gonna turn into a depraved sex maniac! A teenage Jeckle an' Hide. Yo' head is gon' sprout fuzzy like somebody from the Fee-gee Eye-lan's. Yo' hot tongue'll roll out'a your mouth like'a fat snake. You'll pant like'a go-rilla in heat. Yo' buzzooms will blow up like gas balloons an' the nipples will swell an' hang like ripe purple plums. Yo' behin' will begin to work like the ol' gray mare an' you'll strut aroun' flappin' yo' wings like'a raped duck. Then you'll suck me up with one mighty slurp an' fly out'a here a screamin' vampire. They'll finally subdue an' slay you on top'a the Empire State Buildin', with ray guns where you'll be attemptin' to empale yo'self astride that giant antenna. An' nobody will ever know that you, li'l Mary Lou Bolton, who jus' graduated from Elmira College, was lookin' to lay down in front of a big, black bulldozer, to keep America safe for democracy.

Mary Lou
I think I get your point.
> *ELLEN enters.*

Ellen
Mary Lou! Are you coming or not? Everyone's leaving.
> *MARY LOU and ELLEN exit. ELLEN scolding. CORA enters.*

Cora
Shangy! Movin' man's waitin'.
> *SHANTY takes off his apron.*

32

Johnny
Where you think you goin'?

Shanty
Movin' in with Cora today.

Johnny
Not on my time, you ain't! An' me 'spectin' Sweets any minute.

Cora
Wha's so 'portant 'bout that Crane Nigro Shangy's just gotta be here? Or maybe you 'spectin' standin' room for the 'casion?

Johnny
Ain't lettin' him off an' tha's it.

Cora
Jay Cee, why is you so bent'n boun' on breakin' up our li'l club?

Johnny
Somebody's gotta look out for Shangy if he don't.

Cora
What is you talkin' about? Shangy's free, white an' long pass twenty-one! It ain't none'a yo' business what he does outside this bucket'a blood.

Johnny
Well, bitch, I got news for you. I put him in here when none'a these other hunkies 'roun' here would hire him. Talkin' his up 'side the wall talk an' beatin' up they benches.

Cora
Wha's that gotta do with me?

Johnny
Ain't lettin' you or nobody else turn his head but so far. Jus' per-teckin' my interest.

Cora
Ain't gon' let you stan' in my way, Jay Cee. Me an' Shangy took a likin' for one 'nother from the day I walked in here an' foun' you runnin' this place. Up to now they ain't been much happiness in this worl' for neither one of us. But what li'l we got comin', figger we bes' jump on it with all fo' feet.

Johnny
That the way you feel 'bout it, Shanty?

Shanty
33   Man, she's gonna help me git my drums.

Johnny

She ain't gon' do nothin' but turn you into sump'm you don't wanna be.

Cora

What is you talkin' 'bout, fool?

Johnny

This black bitch is gon' turn you into a real white man, Shanty.

Shanty

What??

Cora

You kin quit this nigger today, Honey. We'll manage.

Johnny

You wanna be a white man, Shanty?

Shanty

Knock that stuff off, Johnny! I don't go for it.

Johnny

You think if you git with somebody like Cora, it'll make the whole thing complete, huh?

Cora

Hush up, Jay Cee.

Johnny

Well, it won't. She'll make you so damn white you won't be able to bang two spoons together.

Cora

I'm warnin' you, Jay Cee.

Johnny

An' play the drums? You'll never play no drums.

> CORA *rushes at* JOHNNY. *He catches her arm and throws her to the floor.* SHANTY *is shocked by* JOHNNY's *cruelty. He makes a move to* JOHNNY.

Shanty

Why you—you—you mother fucker!

> JOHNNY *stands ready to throw a punch.* SHANTY *checks himself. Turns away.* CORA *gets to her feet and goes to him. Puts her arm around him. He shuns her. Exits, slowly.*

Cora

Tha's alright, Jay Cee honey. Tha's all right! That day ain't long off, 'fore you gon' git yours. Honey, you gon' git a hurtin' put on you. You gon' git a hurtin' put on you in the place where you do wrong. 34

Johnny

Better wish all that hurtin' on all them Niggers that messed up yo' min'.

>CORA *exits as* GABE *enters.*

Gabe

Dam! What was all that smoke about?

Johnny

Them two ain't got sense nuff to pour piss out'a a boot if the directions was wrote on the heel.

Gabe

You just don't wanna see anybody git any enjoyment out'a life.

Johnny

Bastard's movin' in with her. You dig that?

Gabe   1999003

An' you tried to stop 'em, huh?

>JOHNNY *doesn't answer. Takes bottle of champagne and bucket. Sets it on a table.*

Well, I see you're gittin' ready for the big homecomin', huh?

Johnny

That's right. An' I don't want you goin' into none'a yo' high'n mighty when Sweets git here. Tell you right now he don't go for none of that giddy-up-yippee-yaye shit!

Gabe

Didn't come to stay. Lemme hold some coins! Lan'lord's on my tail.

Johnny

Good.

>JOHNNY *grins. Spreads bills over table.* GABE *picks them up.*

Gabe

You'll git it all back soon's I git me a show.

Johnny

You keepin' a record?

>A *black man enters.*

On yo' way, wine.

Sweets

S'matter, Sonny Boy? Don't you know me?

Johnny

Sweets? Is it really you?

Sweets

35   It's me, all right.

SWEETS *coughs*. JOHNNY *rushes forward. Embraces*
SWEETS.

Johnny

Lock the doors, Gabe. Don't want no innerrupshuns.

GABE *locks the street doors.* JOHNNY *and* SWEETS *box*
playfully.

Sweets

Minute there, was 'bout to go out an' come back in again.

Johnny

Reason I didn't rec'nize you at firs' was, well, I always remember
you bein' 'bout as sharp as a skeeter's peter in the dead'a winter.
Three hundred suits he had, Gabe. Nothin' but the fines' vines.
Never seen so many kicks in one closet. Wasn't a cat in Harlem. . . .

SWEETS *coughs violently.*

Dam! What you doin' 'bout that cough, Sweets?

Sweets

Little souvenir I picked up at the jute mill.

Johnny

Jute mill?

Sweets

Where they make burlap bags at.

Johnny

Pretty rough in Fedsville, huh?

SWEETS *coughs again.*

Meet my man, Gabe.

GABE *and* SWEETS *shake hands.*

Gabe

Pleased to meet you, Mister Crane.

Sweets

Jus' call me Sweets.

Johnny

Brings bottle and two glasses.

Sweets, some'a Pete Zerroni's bes'.

Sweets

Zerroni? You don't mean ol' big fat Pete from up there in the
Bronx?

Johnny

Yeah. He's runnin' everything down here from soup to nuts! But we
gon' change all that, ain't we, Sweets?

JOHNNY *struggles with cork.*

36

Sweets
Sonny Boy, we wasn't much on sendin' kites. Wha's been happenin' since I been in the joint?

Johnny
Jews, Irish an' the Ginees still runnin' things as usual.

Sweets
No. I mean with you, Sonny Boy.

Johnny
Like you know I had a tough gaff gittin' my divorce. Whole thing started when I wanted her to do a little merchandizin' for me. Real Magdaleen, she was! One thing led to 'nother. Boom! Back to mama she went. Had a helluva time gittin' her to sign this joint over to me. Went into my act. Fell down on my duece'a benders. Gave her the ol' routine. Like how the worl' been treatin' us black folk an' everything. . . .
> *He pops cork. Pours. Holds his glass up. The two men clink their glasses.*

Well, look here, Sweets, here's to our li'l piece'a this town.

Sweets
> *Looks into his glass. As JOHNNY sips.*

Speakin'a husslers, Sonny Boy.
> *He coughs. GABE goes to bar. Gets large glass and fills it with champagne.*

You runnin' any kind'a stable?

Johnny
You kiddin', Sweets?
> *Gives GABE a dirty look.*

Sweets
Pushin' or bookin'?

Johnny
Nay, that ain't my stick.

Sweets
Sonny Boy, when I was yo' age, I was into some'a ev'thing.

Johnny
Wish you wouldn't call me that, Sweets! I ain't that little boy runnin' up an' down Saint Nicklas Avenue for you no more.

Sweets
Jus' habit, Johnny. But I sort'a was hopin' you was into sump'm on
37 yo' own, like.

Johnny

Hell! I been tryin' to stay clean. Waitin' on you, man! Like we planned.

Sweets

Well, now! Tha's—tha's what I wanna talk to you 'bout, Sonny Boy.

Johnny

Yes, sir! You still the boss, Sweets. Didn't think you wanted to git into it jus' yet. Figgered we'd have us a few drinks. Talk 'bout ol' times. . . .

Sweets

Sonny Boy!

Johnny

Sir?

Sweets

Firs' off! I gotta tell you I'm th'ough. . . .

Johnny

Whatchu say?

Sweets

Wrappin' it all up for good. . . .

Johnny

Wrappin' what up?

Sweets

The rackets.

Johnny

You gotta be jokin'.

Sweets

Never been no more ser'us in all my life. . . .

Johnny

Sweets, you jus' tired.

Sweets

Don't need no res'. . . .

Johnny

Git yo'self together. . . .

Sweets

My min's made up.

Johnny

Waitin' on you this long, little more ain't gon' kill me.

Sweets

Look, Sonny Boy, it's like this . . .

Johnny

Shut up with that Sonny Boy, shit!

He tries to control himself. GABE *laughs.*

Look, man. You ain't let the slammers psyche you out? That ain't like you. That ain't like you, at all.

He reaches out to touch SWEETS. SWEETS *jerks away.*
JOHNNY *grabs* SWEETS *by the throat violently.*

Mother fucker! I been waitin' on you for ten long-ass years. You ain't gon' cop out on me like this.

Gabe

Moves to contain JOHNNY.

Cut it out, John! Let him alone. Cain't you see the man's sick?

JOHNNY *hits* GABE *in the stomach.* GABE *doubles over. Goes to the floor.*

Johnny

To SWEETS.

What the hell they do to you, huh?

Sweets

What'd who do to me?

Johnny

In the bastille. They did sump'm to you.

Sweets

Nothin' that wasn't already done to me.

SWEETS *moves to* GABE.

You all right, young fella?

Gabe

Yeah—yeah, I—I'm okay.

Sweets

Takes wallet from GABE's *back pocket. Puts it into his own pocket.*

Shouldn'ta mixed in.

He turns back to JOHNNY.

You got the Charlie fever, Johnny. Tha's what you got. I gave it to you. Took yo' chile's min' an' filled it with the Charlie fever. Givin' you a education or teachin' you to dinner-pail, didn't seem to me to be no way for you to grow up an' be respected like'a man. Way we was raised, husslin' an' usin' yo' biscuit to pull quickies was the only way we could feel like we was men. Couldn't copy Charlie's good points an' live like men. So we copied his bad points. That was the way it was with my daddy an' his daddy before him. We just pissed away our lives tryin' to be like bad Charlie. With all our fine clothes

39

an' big cars. All it did was make us hate him all the more an' our-
selves too. Then I tried to go horse-to-horse with 'em up there in
the Bronx. An' ended up with a ten. All because'a the Charlie fever.
I gave you the Charlie fever, Johnny. An' I'm sorry! Seems to me, the
worse sickness'a man kin have is the Charlie fever.

Johnny
> *Glares at SWEETS.*

Git out'a here, Sweets. Goddam you! Git out'a here. 'Fore I kill
you.
> SWEETS *coughs and exits to the street.* JOHNNY *looks
> after him.*

They did sump'm to him. White sons'a bitches. They did sump'm
to him. Sweets don't give up that easy. Charlie fever. Sheeee!

Gabe
Ten years is a long time. An' the man's sick. Anyone kin see that.

Johnny
He could be fakin'. He's into sump'm! Don't want me in on it. He
used to do that to me all the time. He better be fakin'.
> *Brings his arm up to look at his watch.*

Gabe
What? What the hell. . . .
> *He searches frantically in his pockets.*

I'll be goddam.

Johnny
Hell's matter with you?

Gabe
My watch! It's gone.

Johnny
Hell with your watch!

Gabe
It's gone! An' my wallet! The bread you loaned me! It's gone, too.
> JOHNNY *begins to laugh hysterically.*

What the hell's so goddam funny?

Johnny
It's Sweets! The bastard *is* fakin'. He snatched it!
> *Blackout.*

Yahoo! I had it! I was on it! I was into it, babee!

NO PLACE TO BE SOMEBODY

ACT TWO

SCENE ONE

Time: Two days later
Place: The same
Setting: The same
At rise: GABE sits at table. Whisky bottle before him.
He is obviously drunk. He begins to sing an old Prot-
estant hymn.

Gabe
"Whiter than snow, yes!
Whiter than snow!
Now, wash me, and I shall be
Whiter than snow!"
        He chants.
*We moved out of that dirty-black slum!
Away from those dirty-black people!
Who live in those dirty-black hovels,
Amidst all of that garbage and filth!
Away from those dirty-black people,
Who in every way,
Prove daily
They are what they are!
Just dirty-black people!*

*We moved to a house with a fenced-in yard!
To a clean-white neighborhood!*

It had clean-white sidewalks
And clean-white sheets
That hang from clean-white clotheslines to dry!
They were clean-white people!
Who in every way
Prove daily
They are what they are!
Just clean-white people!

Now those clean-white people thought we were
Dirty-black people!
And they treated us like we were
Dirty-black people!
But we stuck it out!
We weathered the storm!
We cleansed and bathed
And tried to be and probably were
Cleaner than most of those clean-white people!
       He sings.
"Break down every idol, cast out every foe!
Oh, wash me and I shall be whiter than snow!"
       He speaks again.
We went to schools that had clean-white
Rooms with clean-white teachers
Who taught us and all of the clean-white
Children how to be clean and white!
       He laughs.
Now, those dirty-black people across
The tracks became angry, jealous and mean!
When they saw us running or skipping or
Hopping or learning with all of those
Clean-white children!

They would catch us alone
When the clean-white children weren't there!
And kick us or slap us and spit
On our clean-white clothes!
Call us dirty-black names
And say that we wanted to be like our clean-white
Neighbors!

But in spite of the kicking, the slapping
The spitting, we were exceedingly glad!

For we knew we weren't trying to be like
Our clean-white neighbors! Most of all,
We were certain we weren't like those
Dirty-black Niggers,
Who lived in hovels, far away across the tracks!
    He sings.
"Whiter than snow! Oh, whiter than snow!
Please wash me, and I shall be whiter than snow!"
    He speaks again.
So we grew up clean and keen!
And all of our clean-white neighbors
Said we had earned the right to go
Out into the clean-white world
And be accepted as clean-white people!
But we soon learned,
The world was not clean and white!
With all of its powders and soaps!
And we learned too that no matter how
Much the world scrubbed,
The world was getting no cleaner!

Most of all!
We saw that no matter how much or how
Hard we scrubbed,
It was only making us blacker!
So back we came to that dirty-black slum!
To the hovels, the filth and the garbage!
Came back to those dirty-black people!
Away from those clean-white people!
That clean, white anti-septic world!
That scrubs and scrubs and scrubs!

But those dirty-black people!
Those dirty-black people!
Were still angry, jealous and mean!
They kicked us and slapped us and spit again
On our clothes!
Denied us!
Disowned us
And cast us out!
And we still were exceedingly glad!

For at last they knew
47 We were not like our clean-white neighbors!

Most of all! We were safe!
Assured at last!
We could never more be
Like those dirty-black Niggers!
Those filthy, dirty-black Niggers!
Who live far away!
Far away, in hovels across the tracks!
>   *He bursts into song.*
"Whiter than snow! Yes! Whiter than snow!
Oh, wash me and I shall be whiter than snow!"

>   GABE *is on his knees. Hands stretched up to heaven. Lights*
>   *slowly dim out on him, and come up on bar.* SHANTY *is*
>   *behind the bar.* MIKE MAFFUCCI *stands at center, throw-*
>   *ing darts into a dartboard.* SWEETS CRANE *enters.*

Shanty
Hit the wind, Mac. This ain't the place.

Sweets
Johnny here?

Shanty
What you want with Johnny?

Sweets
I'm a frien'a his.

Shanty
Yeah? Well, he ain't here.

Sweets
Where's me a broom an' a drop pan?

Shanty
What for?

Sweets
Need me a bucket an' some rags too.

Shanty
What do you want all that shit for?

Sweets
The floor, they don't look too good an' the windas, it could stan'. . . .

Shanty
Eighty-six, ol' timer! We ain't hirin'.

Sweets
Ain't askin' f'no pay.

Shanty
What'a ya? Some kind'a nut? C'mon! Out you go. Eighty-six.   48

Sweets

Think you better wait till Johnny gets here. Let him put me out.

> SWEETS *pushes* SHANTY *roughly aside and moves to kitchen.*

Think I'll fin' what I need back here.

Shanty

> *Looks incredulous. Scratches his head and follows* SWEETS *to kitchen.*
> JOHNNY *enters.* SHANTY *rushes in from kitchen.*

Hey, Johnny! Some ol' timer just came in an'. . . .

Maffucci

How you doin', Johnny Cake?

Johnny

> *Stops short.*

Only one cat usta call me that.

Maffucci

Gettin' warm, Johnny Cake.

Johnny

> *Moves behind bar.*

Little snotty-nose wop kid, name Mike Maffucci.

Maffucci

On the nose.

> *Sends a dart in* JOHNNY's *direction.* JOHNNY *ducks. The dart buries into the wood of the back bar. Both men laugh. They shake hands.*

Long time no see, eh, Johnny Cake?

Johnny

What you drinkin'?

Maffucci

Little dago red. Gotta take it easy on my stomach with the hard stuff.

> JOHNNY *snaps his fingers.* SHANTY *brings bottle.*

Shanty

Dig, Johnny! Some ol' goat. . . .

Johnny

Cool it, Shanty. Can't you see I'm busy? How's your ol' man, Footch?

Maffuci

> *Makes the sign of the cross.*

My ol' man chalked out, Johnny. Heart attack. Right after you went to the nursery. You ain't still sore 'bout what happened, are you, Johnny Cake?

49

Johnny

Bygones is bygones, Footch!

Maffucci

Glad'a hear ya say that, Johnny. Didn't know what happened to you after that. When they tole me you was runnin' this joint, had'a come over an' see ya.

> *He looks around. SWEETS enters with broom and rags. Proceeds to sweep the floor. JOHNNY registers surprise and anger. SHANTY starts to say something but JOHNNY puts his finger to his lips.*

How ya doin' with the place, Johnny?

Johnny

Stabbin' horses to steal blankets. Jay Cee ag'inst the worl'.

Maffucci

Joe Carneri used to say that. You ain't never forgot that huh, Johnny?

> *JOHNNY glances angrily at SWEETS.*

Remember the first time they busted him? There was this pitchure on the front page. Joe's standin' on the courthouse steps. Cops an' reporters all aroun'. Joe's yellin' "Jay Cee ag'inst the worl'! Jay Cee ag'inst the worl'!"

Johnny

He sho' was your hero all right.

Maffucci

Too bad he had'a go an' git hit like that. Sittin' in a barber chair!

Johnny

Better'n the electric chair.

> *SWEETS is now dusting the chairs.*

Maffucci

You know, Johnny Cake, that was a groovy idea for a kid! Coppin' all that scrapiron from ol' Julio an' then sellin' it back to him.

> *He breaks up laughing.*

Johnny

Wasn't so pretty when I tried to tell the fuzz you was in on it with me.

Maffucci

Awful sorry 'bout that, Johnny Cake.

> *MAFFUCCI puts his hand on JOHNNY's shoulder. JOHNNY knocks his hand off. MAFFUCCI comes down on JOHNNY's shoulder with a karate chop. JOHNNY punches MAFFUCCI in the stomach and shoves him away. Comes toward MAFFUCCI menacingly. SWEETS keeps sweeping.* 50

Johnny

One thing I gotta give you Ginees credit for. Sho' know how to stick together when you wanna.

Maffucci

> *Backs away.*

He was my father, Johnny. Any father would'a done the same thing. If he had the connections.

Johnny

Who tole you I was runnin' this joint, Footch?

Maffucci

To give you the works, Johnny, I'm one'a Pete Zerroni's local boys now.

> SWEETS *dusts near* MAFFUCCI.

Johnny

No jive! Battin' in the big leagues, ain't you? Your ol' man was aroun', bet he'd be pretty proud'a you.

Maffucci

Would you believe, my ol' man had ideas 'bout me bein' a lawyer or a doctor?

Johnny

What you doin' for Pete?

Maffucci

Sort'a community relations like, Johnny.

Johnny

> *Laughs.*

I'm one'a Pete's customers! What kind'a community relashuns you got for me?

Maffucci

Glad you opened that, Johnny Cake. Pete says you got him a little concerned.

Johnny

What is he, crazy? Ain't he got more 'portant things on his min'?

Maffucci

Way we got it, first thing ol' Sweets Crane did when he got out was come see you.

Johnny

So what? Sweets was like'a father to me.

Maffucci

So I hear. But before they shut the gate on him, he let some things drop. Like, he made a few threats. What I hear 'bout him, might be crazy enough to give 'em a try.

JOHNNY *laughs.*

What, am I throwin' zingers or sump'm? What's the joke?

Johnny

Sweets came 'roun' to tell me he's all caught up.

Maffucci

Wouldn't promote me, would you, Johnny Cake? For ol' time's sake, let's not you an' me go horse-to-horse 'bout nothin'.

Johnny

On the up an' up, Footch. Sweets has wrapped it all up for good. Matter'a fack, right now he's doin' odd gigs an' singin' the straight an' narrow.

Maffucci

Wanna believe you, Johnny. But just in case you an' this Sweets are thinkin' 'bout makin' a little noise, Pete wants me to give you the six-to-five!

SWEETS *bumps into* MAFFUCCI, *spilling the wine down the front of* MAFFUCCI's *suit.*

Hey! Watch it there, pops!

Sweets

Awful sorry 'bout that, mister!

Attempts to wipe MAFFUCCI's *suit with the rag.* MAF-FUCCI *pushes him aside.*

Maffucci

That's okay, pops!

SWEETS *continues to wipe* MAFFUCCI's *vest.*

Okay, okay, I said!

SWEETS *stops, and continues with his work.*

Well, Johnny Cake. Like to stay an' rap with ya a little bit but you know how it is. Community relations.

Johnny

Sho' preshiate you lookin' out for me, Footch!

Maffucci

Think nothin' of it, Johnny Cake. It's Pete. He don't like jigs. Says the minute they git a little somethin', they start actin' cute. You an' me, we was like brothers. Way I see it, was like you took a dive for me once. Figger I owe ya.

Johnny

You don't owe me a dam thing, Footch.

52

Maffucci
> *Heads for the street doors. Turns back.*

You know, Johnny Cake, some reason I never been able to git you off my mind. After all these years. I think if you'da been a wop, you'da been a big man in the rackets.
> *Exits.* SWEETS *holds watch to ear.*

Johnny
All right now, Sweets. Goddamit, wha's this game you playin'?

Shanty
Sweets??? That's Sweets Crane?

Johnny
Shut up, Shanty.
> *Snatches the rag out of* SWEETS' *hand. Gets broom. Gives both to* SHANTY.

Take this crap back to the kitchen.
> SHANTY *takes them to kitchen.*

Man, you either gotta be stir-buggy or you puttin' on one helluva ack.

Sweets
> *Checks the watch.*

Jus' tryin' to be helpful, Sonny Boy.

Johnny
Don't you be kickin' no more farts at me, man. Wha's with this pil'fin stuff off'a people an' makin' like'a dam lackey? You mus' be plumb kinky.

Sweets
Cain't see no point in watchin' George Raff on tee vee ev'a night. All my life I been into things. Always active.

Johnny
This what you call bein' active? An' look at you! Look like you jus' come off the Bow'ry! Ain't they no pride lef' in you?

Sweets
Pride? Sheee. Pride, Sonny Boy, is sump'm I ain't got no mo' use for.

Johnny
For the las' time, ol' man. You better tell me wha's happenin' with you. Don't you make me have to kill you.

Sweets
> *Produces an envelope.*

I'm as good as dead right now!
> *He hands* JOHNNY *the envelope.*

Johnny
53 What the hell is it?

Sweets
Guess you could call it my will.

Johnny
> *Turns it over.*

Yo' will??

Sweets
Open it up.

Johnny
Shanty!

Shanty
> *Enters.*

How ya doin', Sweets?

Johnny
Check this out, Shanty. I don't read this jive so good.

Shanty
> *Reads will.*

It's legal stuff. Says here you're gonna inherit interest in barbershops, meat markets, stores an' a whole lotta Harlem real estate. Dam!

Johnny
> *Snatches the papers out of SHANTY's hands.*

You gotta be jokin'.

Sweets
I'm leavin' it all to you, Sonny Boy. My lawyers will take care ev'thing.

Johnny
How come you ain't tole me nothin' 'bout this before?

Sweets
Couldn't take no chance it gittin' out. Might'a strung me out on a tax rap too.

Johnny
You lookin' to take some kind'a back gate commute? Suicide?

Sweets
> *Coughs.*

Doctors ain't gimme but six months to ride. Didn't wanna lay it on you till they made sho'.

Johnny
Six months, huh?

Sweets
Mo' or less.

Johnny
Goddamit, Sweets. What the hell kin I say? I sho' been a real bastard.
Guess it don't help none for me to say I'm sorry.

Sweets
Might he'p some if you was to turn all this into sump'm worth while
an' good. Maybe the Lawd will f'give me f'the way I got it.
> *Bursts into laughter and coughs.*

Johnny
Git off it, Sweets. Jus' 'cause you s'pose to chalk out on us don't mean
you gotta go an' 'brace relijun.

Sweets
Figure it won't hurt none if I do.

Johnny
Shit. That good Lawd you talkin' 'bout is jus' as white as that judge
who sent yo' black ass to Fedsville.

Sweets
How you know? You ever seen him? When I was down there in that
prison, I reads a lot. Mos'ly the Bible. Bible tells me, the Lawd was
hard to look upon. Fack is, he was so hard to look upon that nobody
eva looked at him an' lived. Well, I got to figgerin' on that. An' reasons
that was so, 'cause he was so black.
> *Goes into loud laughter and coughs again.*

Lawd knows! White's easy nuff to look at!
> JOHNNY *throws the will on the floor.* SWEETS *goes to*
> *his knees and clutches the will.*

What you doin', Sonny Boy? My life is in them papers!
> *Hits* JOHNNY *with hat.* JOHNNY *reaches under the bar*
> *and comes up with a revolver. Levels it at* SWEETS.

Johnny
See this, Sweets? My firs' an' only pistol. You gave it to me long time
ago when I was a lookout for you when you was pullin' them owl jobs
in Queens. I worshipped the groun' you walked on. I thought the sun
rose an' set in yo' ass. You showed me how to make thirteen straight
passes without givin' up the dice. Stood behin' me an' nudged me
when to play my ace. Hipped me how to make a gapers cut. How to
handle myself in a pill joint. Taught me to trust no woman over six or
under sixty. Turned me on to the best horse players an' number run-
ners. Showed me how to keep my ass-pocket full'a coins without goin'
to jail. Said the wors' crime I ever committed was comin' out'a my
mama screamin' black. Tole me all about white folks an' what to ex-
55   pect from the best of 'em. You said as long as there was a single

white man on this earth, the black man only had one free choice. That was the way he died. When you went to jail for shootin' Cholly you said, "Sonny Boy, git us a plan." Well, I got us a plan. Now, you come back here nutty an' half dead, dancin' all over me about me goin' through a change'a life. An' how you want me to help you git ready to meet yo' Lawd. Well, git ready, mother fucker. Tha's exactly what I'm gon' do. Help you to meet him.

> JOHNNY *pulls back the hammer of the gun.* SWEETS *coughs and looks at the barrel of the gun.*

Sweets
You ain't gon' shoot me, Johnny. You cain't shoot me. They's a whole lotta you I ain't even touched.

> SWEETS *exits. Blackout.*

SCENE TWO

Time: Two weeks later
Place: The same
Setting: The same
At rise: GABE sits at a table. Glass of red wine before him, strumming a guitar. MELVIN stands next to him thumbing through a playscript. SHANTY is behind the bar as usual.

Melvin

"The Tooth of a Red Tiger"? What part will you play, Gabe?

Gabe

What you tryin' to do, Mel? Jinx me? I ain't got the part yet.

Melvin

They gave you this script, didn't they?

Gabe

The part calls for a guitar player. Cain't you hear these clinkers?

MELVIN puts script on table.

How was your recital?

Melvin

Ugh! Don't remind me, Gabe. I have this solo in "variations and diversions." I have to do three tour jêtés? Well, ol' Mel fell! Would you believe it? I stumbled and fell! Victor, my teacher, he was there shaking! He was actually shaking.

Gabe

What the hell, Mel. Always another recital.

57

Melvin
I suppose you could look at it that way! Anyway, I was simply heartbroken. Gabe, do you like Carl Sandburg?

Gabe
Ain't exactly in love with him.

Melvin
I was thinking, since you do write poetry, maybe you'd like to go with me to hear some of his works. Peter Demeter is reading tomorrow night. . . .

Gabe
Got somethin' I gotta do.

Melvin
Well, maybe you'd like to hear some chamber music at the Brooklyn Academy over the weekend.

Gabe
Don't dig chamber music, Mel.

Melvin
I believe an artist should learn all he can about the other forms too.
          Slaps GABE on his back and exits to kitchen.

Dee
          Enters and goes to the bar.
Squeeze the bar rag out, Shanty.
          She glances at GABE.
Full of little surprises, aren't you?

Gabe
Just fakin'.
          SHANTY pours her drink. She takes bottle and glass to a table. Suddenly she catches GABE staring at her.

Dee
What's with the fish eyes? I gotta new wrinkle or sump'm?

Gabe
Sorry! Just thinkin'!

Dee
          Downs drink.
You think too much! Give it a rest!

Gabe
Tell me somethin', Dee . . .

Dee
What'a ya? Writin' a book or sump'm?   58

Gabe

How'd you meet up with John in the first place?

Dee

> *Doesn't answer. Pours another drink. Presently gets to her feet. Goes to window. Peers out.*

Got Evie to thank for that. She used to come in here a lot when the joint was really jumpin'. She'll never admit it but I think she had it for Johnny. She's never been much of a drinker but one night she got too looped to drive. Johnny brought her home. When they came in, I was in the process of having my face lifted by a boyfriend. Johnny pulled him off.

Gabe

Stop me if I'm bein' a little too personal.

Dee

Oh, you be as personal as you like, Gabe.

Gabe

How do chicks like you an' Evie . . .

Dee

Get into the life? Is that what you're askin'? For me it was easy! Got a job as a sales girl! Rich Johns would come in propositioning the girls! One day I took one up on it, and here I am.

Gabe

Was it for the money?

Dee

What cheap paperbacks you been readin', Gabe?

Gabe

I get it! You hate your father.

Dee

That poor miserable bastard? That bum? He ain't worth hating.

Gabe

You love John?

Dee

Johnny? Johnny's not the kind of man you love. I think I pity Johnny. Don't get me wrong. I don't mean the kind of pity you'd give to my father or some bum on the street. Somebody blindfolded him. Turned him around. Somewhere inside Johnny's got something. It just come out crooked! Comes out the wrong way.

> *She takes drink and becomes theatrical.*

59   In a way, Johnny reminds me of a classmate of mine in high school.

Gabe

Boyhood sweetheart, huh?

Dee

Got me pregnant. Nice decent boy. Only, he was black. Went to my folks. Said, "I'll marry her." The crazy bastard. They made his life miserable. I don't have to tell you.

Gabe

Did you love this boy?

Dee

You mean, why didn't we run away together? We were too young and stupid.

Gabe

And the baby?

Dee

Oh, they got rid of it for me.
> *She almost appears to be improvising.*

Word got out somehow. My mother fled to Puerto Rico for a well needed vacation. I stayed around the house.
> *She lapses into theatrical Southern dialect à la Tennessee Williams.*

For weeks I just read, listened to the radio or watched television. One night late my father came in dead drunk. Staggered into my room and got into bed with me. Week later, I came to New York.
> *She giggles.*

Funny thing. When I first got into the life, I was always thinkin' about my father. He was always comin' into my mind. Like it was him I was screwin' over and over again. Like I was takin' him away from my mother and punishin' him for lettin' her rule his life.

Gabe

You know? Just the way you're standin' there, you remind me of somebody?

Dee

Dame May Whitty?

Gabe

Maxine.

Dee

Who?

Gabe

Maxine.

Dee

Who's Maxine?

Gabe

Probably every woman I've ever known.

Dee

I don't usually think of you with a woman.

Gabe

Come on, Dee!

Dee

I didn't mean it like that, Gabe. I always think of you—well, sort'a like the intellectual type! For some reason people kind'a think intellectual types don't even use the toilet! So who's Maxine?

Gabe

My mother.

Dee

Talking to you is like eatin' cotton candy.

Gabe

She was the little girl who sat across from me.

Dee

In grade school?

Gabe

I stole a quarter from her. It was in her inkwell. Teacher lined us up. Searched us. The quarter rolled out of the pocket of my hightop boots. I kin still hear them kids yellin' "Our theeefer!"

Dee

Pretty humiliatin', huh?

Gabe

We sang duets together in the high school choir. Neck an' rub stomachs in dark alleys an' doorways. They kicked her out'a school when she got pregnant. Sent her away. They was sure I did it. Her mama was wild an' crazy. Turned tricks for a cat who owned a Cadillac. Didn't want me messin' aroun' with Maxine. Said I was a dicty Nigger an' jus' wanted Maxine's ass. When Maxine didn't make her period, her mama got drunk an' come lookin' for me with a razor. I hid out for a couple days. Heard later she slashed all the upholsterin' in her pimp's Cadillac. Ha! She was smart, Maxine was. An' Jewish too. Taught me social consciousness. Said I was a good lover. Said white boys got their virility in how much money they made an' the kind'a car they drove. Said I related better 'cause I was black an' had nothin' to offer but myself. So I quit my job. Used to

61

hide in the closet when her folks came in from Connecticut. Listened to 'em degradin' her for livin' with an' supportin' a Nigger. Maxine got herself an Afro hair-do an' joined the Black Nationalists when I couldn't afford to get her hair straightened at Rose Meta's! Didn't really wanna marry me. Jus' wanted my baby so she could go on welfare. She is out there somewhere. Maxine is. She's out there, waitin' on me to come back to her, Maxine is.

Dee
> *Laughs.*

Gabe? Gabe, are you sure you're all right?
> *He grins.*

You really loved Maxine, didn't you?
> *She puts her arms around his neck.*

Gabe
I sure wanted to . . .

Johnny
> *Enters.*

What the hell's goin' on here?

Gabe
You jealous?

Johnny
Depen's on yo' intenshuns.
> GABE *puts guitar into case. Picks up script. Prepares to leave.*

Johnny
What, you done gone an' got yo'self a job an' ain't tole nobody?

Gabe
It's only an audition.

Dee
Good luck, Gabe.

Johnny
Yeah. I'm lookin' forward to gettin' a few payments back on all them loans.
> GABE *gives a razz-berry and exits.*

You know, Dee? I been thinking. Maybe we ought'a take that trip after all.

Dee
Well now, you don't say? Sweets Crane wouldn't have anything to do with this sudden change of mind, would he?
> *She starts to pour another drink.*

62

Johnny
> *Snatches bottle out of her hands.*

Take it easy on that stuff, girl! Still wanna go, don't you?

Dee
Right now I got somethin' more important on my mind.

Johnny
Dump it on me.

Dee
I want out of the life, Johnny.

Johnny
Dam! You are stoned, ain't you?

Dee
I mean it, Johnny.

Johnny
Thought you an' me had a understandin'.

Dee
There's a hell of a lot more room for a better one.

Johnny
Like what, for instance?

Dee
I need some permanence.

Johnny
You mean git married?

Dee
Maybe.

Johnny
Thought you was down on all that housewife jazz.

Dee
I don't take tee vee commercials very seriously if that's what you mean.

Johnny
I gotta business here! Tough nuff time keepin' it perm'nant! Wasn't for the coins you bring in, I'd go under 'fore the week was out.

Dee
Let's build it back up, Johnny. Together. Together, Johnny.

Johnny
What the hell you know 'bout this business?

Dee
63 Teach me, Johnny! You could teach me.

Johnny

No good. Ain't no woman'a mine gon' be workin'. She b'long at home.
>*She laughs.*

Look'a here, go on home. Git yo'self together. We'll talk 'bout it later.

Dee

I'll tie a string around my finger.
>*She gathers her things. Weaves to the street door.*

Johnny

Hey, girl! You still ain't said where you wanna go.

Dee

>*Whirls.*

I don't know. I hear the north pole's pretty swingin' these days.

Johnny

Keep it up. I'll break yo' damn chops yet.

Dee

Where thou goest, I will follow, Johnny baby.

Johnny

Thinkin' 'bout makin' the Bim'ni scene. Won't have to worry 'bout crackers doin' the bird with the long red neck. Split this weekend. You make res'vashuns.

Dee

>*Blows him a kiss. Bows theatrically.*

Yah suh, Boss!
>*She exits.*

Johnny

Bitches. Cain't please none of 'em.
>*Blackout.*

SCENE THREE

Time: A day later
Place: The same
Setting: The same
At rise: MELVIN *is arranging chairs and straightening tablecloths.* GABE *enters.*

Melvin
What happened, Gabe? Did you get the part?

Gabe
Nah! Wasn't the right type after all.

Melvin
What type did they want?

Gabe
Whatever it was I wasn't it.

Johnny
> *Enters from kitchen. He is munching a sandwich.*
Nigra type.

Melvin
What type is that?

Johnny
Whatever it is, tha's what he ain't.

Melvin
Doesn't talent have anything to do with it?

65

Johnny

Prop'ganda, Mel! When whitey pick one'a y'all you gotta either be a clown, a freak or a Nigra type.

Gabe

They do the same thing among themselves too.

Johnny

'Mongst themselves, they ain't so damn choosey.

Gabe

Should'a seen the cat they did pick. Hell, I'm as black as he is.

Johnny

Gabe, ain't they no mirrors in yo' house?

Gabe

I mean black in here!

Melvin

You people are more preoccupied with color than white people are.

Johnny

They won't let us be porcupined with nothin' else.

Gabe

Don't make no difference what color I am. I'm still black.

Johnny

Yeah! But you ain't gon' git no chance to prove it. Not on no stage, you ain't. You remin' whitey'a too many things he don't wanna take'a look at. Figgers he's got nuff problems dealin' with Niggers who jus' look black, like me.

Gabe

Aw, shut the fuck up, John.

Johnny

Who you talkin' to?

Gabe

You, you bastard. I'm tellin' you to shut the fuck up. Jus' cool it with yo' shit.

Johnny

Jus' tryin' to tell you like it is, Gabe! You jus' don't b'lieve a hard head makes a sof' ass!

Melvin

> *Pats GABE on the back.*

Like you told me, Gabe. Always another recital.

> MELVIN *exits to kitchen.* JOHNNY *tosses* GABE *some bills.*

66

Gabe
No more handouts, baby.

Johnny
This ain't no handout! Want you to do me a favor.

Gabe
Yeah?

Johnny
Me an' Dee goin' on a little vacation. Want you to help Shanty an' Mel with the store while we gone.

Gabe
When you leavin'?

Johnny
End'a the week. Makin' it to Bim'ni.
>CORA *and* SHANTY *enter. Carry black drum cases.*

Cora
Give us a han' here, Gabe? They's more out there in the cab.
>GABE *exits to the street.*

Johnny
What you bringin' this junk in here for?

Cora
We bringin' this junk in here as you call it on a purpose.

Johnny
Be damned if tha's so. Git out'a here, an' Shanty, lets git to work.
>GABE *returns with another case.*

Cora
Look'a here, Jay Cee. Me an' Shangy swore when we got these here drums, we was gon' bring 'em in here for you to look at an' lissen to with yo' own eyes an' ears.

Johnny
All of a sudden I done gone deaf an' blin'. Now, git this hazarae out'a here.

Cora
Ain't gon' do ner such thing. Not till me an' Shangy has got som'a what we's set out to do.

Gabe
Sure got a pretty good start.

Cora
Shangy! What is you doin' with the broom?
>JOHNNY *reaches for one of the drum cases.*

Take yo' nasty, stinkin', filthy black han's off them drums!
> JOHNNY *recoils.*

Melvin
> *Comes out of the kitchen.*
What on earth is happening?

Cora
It ain't happenin' yet.

Melvin
Well, I just never would have believed it. Isn't it wonderful?

Cora
'Fore Shangy gits on these drums, they's sump'm you oughta know, Jay Cee.

Johnny
You runnin' the show.

Cora
Shangy is quittin' you today. Right now.

Johnny
Why the hell didn't you say that in the first place?

Cora
'Cause you was so busy gittin' these drums out'a here. Tha's why.

Melvin
You're really going to play for us, Shanty?

Cora
Tha's his intenchun, thank you. Shangy! Will you come on over here? Gabe don't know nothin' 'bout what he's doin'.
> SHANTY *hands* JOHNNY *the broom. Approaches the drums reluctantly.*

Johnny
Some reason, Shangy, you don't look so happy. Now I want you to jump up there an' give ol' Jay Cee a little wham-bam-thank-ya-ma'm. Piece'a the funky nitty-gritty. Like the time they said you played like'a spade. Guess I kin risk gittin' a summons on that.

Cora
Ne' min', Jay Cee. Go 'head, honey! Git yo'se'f together. Take all the time you need.

Gabe
Wail, baby.
> SHANTY *sits on the stool. Fumbles. Accidentally puts foot on pedal. Strikes pose. Taps cymbals. Moves to*　68

snares. Mixes. Pumps. Works. Gets loud. CORA fidgets. Anxious. SHANTY fakes. Can't cover up. Becomes frustrated. Louder. Stands. Begins to beat wildly. Moves around the drums banging for all he's worth. CORA is ashamed. GABE frowns. CORA grabs SHANTY's arm. He pushes her away. Becomes a windmill.

Cora

Stop it, Shangy! Stop it, I said!

SHANTY beats as if possessed. CORA is helpless. JOHNNY calmly reaches behind the bar. Gets pitcher of water. Pours it over SHANTY's head.

Shanty

Ya-hoooo!

Leaps into the air.

I had it! I was on it! I was into it, babee!

He moves around doing the pimp walk.

Ol' Red Taylor said I had the thing. Said, "Shanty man! You got the thing!"

Goes to MEL.

Gimme some skin, mother fucker.

MEL gives him some skin. Goes to GABE.

Gimme some skin.

GABE doesn't put his hand out.

Ah, fuck you, man. Didn't I hip you to my happenin's, Johnny? Didn't I show you where it's at?

Johnny

You burned, baby, you burned.

SHANTY gives JOHNNY some skin.

Cora

Shangy! I—think you better start packin' up now.

Shanty

Git away from me, you funky black bitch.

Cora

Shangy!

Shanty

Just stay away from me—you evil piece'a chunky.

Cora

You ain't got no call to say nothin' like that to me.

Shanty

Oh, no? You ain't jive timin' me, you just like Gloria.

69

Cora
What you sayin', Shangy?

Shanty
You don't want me to play no drums.

Cora
You wrong, Shangy.

Shanty
Thought you'd make a fool out'a me, did you? Gittin' me to bring these drums in here. You thought I'd mess it up. Well, I showed you where it was at. I showed all'a you.

Cora
Shangy, you crazy! You the one suggestid that!

Shanty
Bitch, call the man. Have him come git these drums.

Cora
Come git the drums? Why, Shangy? Why?

Shanty
I don't need you to help me get my drums. I get my own drums. Dig it?

Cora
This chile done clean los' his min'.

Shanty
You an' me are through! Dig it? We are through. We've had it. Splitsville.
>   CORA *is numb.*
Now you believe me huh, Johnny? A bucket'a cold water an' throw it on me, huh?

Johnny
To git you to quit. Come on, baby. Let's git some dry clothes on you.
>   JOHNNY *leads* SHANTY *to the kitchen.*

Shanty
A bucket'a cold water like the night we played "Saints" . . .
>   JOHNNY *and* SHANTY *exit to kitchen. For a moment*
>   CORA *looks up at the clock.*

Cora
What time is it, Gabe?

Gabe
My watch was stolen . . .

70

Cora
> *Points to clock above cash register.*

What time do that clock say?

Gabe

Quarter after three . . .

Cora

Know sump'm, Gabe? I ain't never learned how to tell time. Thirty years ol' an' I don't even know the time'a day. But when I gits up in the mornin', tha's the very firs' thing I'm gon' do. I'm gonna learn how to tell me some time.
> *She exits.*

Johnny
> *Enters from kitchen.*

Go back there an' help Shanty, Mel! He don't feel so good.
> MELVIN *goes to kitchen.*

Help me tear down this thing, Gabe.
> JOHNNY *begins to dismantle drums.*

Gabe

Do it your damned-self. I ain't feelin' so hot either.
> *Exits hurriedly.*

Johnny

Now, what in hell's matter with you?
> *Busies himself with the drums.* MARY LOU BOLTON *enters.*

Mary Lou

Hello . . .

Johnny
> *His attention is still with the drums.*

Sump'm I kin do for you?

Mary Lou
> *Moves to table. Sits.*

I'd like a daiquiri, please.

Johnny
> *Looks up.*

Tha's one drink I ain't never been able to make right.

Mary Lou

Simple! Just go easy with the sugar.

Johnny
> *Goes behind bar. Begins to mix drink. Dumps in a lot of sugar.*

71 Never 'spected to see you back here ag'in.

Mary Lou

Let's just say, I don't scare so easy. By the way, what were you trying to prove anyway?

Johnny

> *Comes to her table and sets the drink before her.*

I was waitin' for you to ask sump'm like that.

Mary Lou

Really?

Johnny

You sho' didn't come back here for no drink.

Mary Lou

Pretty conceited, aren't you?

Johnny

Jus' hipt to yo' kin', tha's all.

Mary Lou

"My kind," huh?

Johnny

You don't like to be kept in the dark 'bout nothin'.

Mary Lou

That's the difference between man and beast.

Johnny

I kin see you ain't learned a damned thing in that college, neither.

Maffucci

> *Enters with truck driver who carries case of whisky to kitchen.*

How you doin', Johnny Cake?

Johnny

Okay, Gumba. What'd Pete do? Demote you? Got you ridin' the truck.

Maffucci

New kind'a community relations, Johnny Cake. Ride aroun' with the boys, see if the customers are happy. You happy, Johnny Cake?

> *Truck driver comes out of kitchen, exits.*

Johnny

Dee-leer-iuss.

Maffucci

> *Spies MARY LOU.*

Good, good. Makes me happy too.

> *He moves to MARY LOU.*

Say! Ain't you Judge Bolton's kid?

72

Mary Lou
Why, yes. Yes I am.

Maffucci
> *Takes her in his arms. Handles her. She resists, to no avail.*
Never forget a face. Turned out to be a real nice tomata, huh? Don't mind me, kid.
> *He releases her.*
Next time you see your ol' man, tell him Mike Maffucci says "Hello!"
> *He pats her on the behind.*
See you aroun', Johnny Cake!
> *Looks at drums. Taps them.*
Didn't know you was rhythmical.

Johnny
> JOHNNY *reacts playfully by toying with the drum sticks.*
Chow, Footch.
> MAFFUCCI *exits.*
Okay. How does he know yo' ol' man?

Mary Lou
> *Visibly shaken.*
They were clients of his.

Johnny
They? They who? You mean Footch?

Mary Lou
> *Nods.*
Something about bribing a city official. And someone was murdered.

Johnny .
Mary. Does the name Pete Zerroni ring a bell?

Mary Lou
Yes! He was one of the defendants. My father won the case.

Johnny
I don't care what nobody say. Your father was a damn good lawyer.

Mary Lou
What's your interest? You know this Pete Zerroni?

Johnny
Not personal.

Mary Lou
73 He's not a very good person to know.

Johnny

With Pete, sometimes you ain't got no choice.

> *She prepares to leave.*

Here! Lemme freshen up yo' drink.

Mary Lou

No thanks. I'm getting—I'm getting a headache.

> *She moves to the street doors.*

Goodbye, mister . . .

Johnny

Johnny. Johnny Williams.

Mary Lou

Goodbye, Johnny. . . .

> *She exits, leaving her purse.*

Johnny

> *Picks her purse up. Thinks for a moment. Goes to phone, dials.*

Hey, Dee? Cancel them reservashuns. Sump'm important jus' came up. Won't be able to after all. Now don't hand me no crap. Just cancel.

> *Blackout.*

You'd'a made out better as a cook, Pops. Mama couldn't beat that macaroni salad!

NO PLACE
TO BE
SOMEBODY

ACT THREE

SCENE ONE

Time: Two weeks later
Place: The same
Setting: The same
At rise: Table at center has a folded newspaper leaning
against a large Molotov cocktail. Its headline reads:
"Negroes Riot!" A banner resembling the American flag
dangles from a flagstand. Next to the Molotov cocktail
is a plate, on which rests a large black automatic pistol. Be-
side the plate is a knife and fork. A toilet is heard flushing. GABE comes on stage zipping his pants. His attitude
is ceremonial.

Gabe
"They's mo' to bein' black than meets the
    Eye!
Bein' black, is like the way ya walk an'
    Talk!
It's a way'a lookin' at life!
Bein' black, is like sayin', "Wha's happenin',
    Babeee!"
An' bein' understood!
Bein' black has a way'a makin' ya call some-
Body a mu-tha-fuc-kah, an' really meanin' it!
An' namin' eva'body broh-thah, even if you don't!
Bein' black, is eatin' chit'lins an' wah-tah-

Melon, an' to hell with anybody, if they don't
Like it!
Bein' black has a way'a makin' ya wear bright
Colors an' knowin' what a fine hat or a good
Pair'a shoes look like an' then—an' then—
It has a way'a makin' ya finger pop! Invent a
New dance! Sing the blues! Drink good Scotch!
Smoke a big seegar while pushin' a black Cadil-
lac With white sidewall tires! It's conkin' yo'
Head! Wearin' a black rag to keep the wave!
Carryin' a razor! Smokin' boo an' listenin' to
Gut-bucket jazz!
Yes! They's mo' to bein' black than meets the eye!
Bein' black is gittin' down loud an' wrong! Uh-huh!
It's makin' love without no hangups! Uh-huh! Or
Gittin' sanctified an' holy an' grabbin' a han'ful'a
The sistah nex' to ya when she starts speakin' in
Tongues!
Bein' black is havin' yo' palm read! Hittin' the
Numbers! Workin' long an' hard an' gittin' the
Short end'a the stick an' no glory! It's
Knowin' they ain't no dif'rence 'tween
White trash an' white quality! Uh-huh!
Bein' black is huggin' a fat mama an' hav-
in' her smell like ham-fat, hot biscuits
An' black-eyed peas!
Yes! They's mo' to bein' black than meets
The eye!   .
Bein' black has a way'a makin' ya mad mos'
Of the time, hurt all the time an' havin'
So many hangups, the problem'a soo-side
Don't even enter yo' min'! It's buyin'
What you don't want, beggin' what you don't
Need! An' stealin' what is yo's by rights!
Yes! They's mo' to bein' black than meets the
Eye!
It's all the stuff that nobody wants but
Cain't live without!
It's the body that keeps us standin'! The
Soul that keeps us goin'! An' the spirit
That'll take us thooo!
Yes! They's mo' to bein' black than meets
The eye!''

> GABE *sits at table. Cuts into gun with knife and fork.*
> *Finally picks gun up. Bites into it. Chews and swallows.*
> *Takes drink from Molotov cocktail. Wipes mouth.*

Bru-thas an' sistahs! Will ya jine me!

> *Blackout on* GABE. *Lights come up on* DEE *and* SHANTY.
> *She sits at table, bottle of whisky in front of her.* SHANTY
> *sits on stool reading copy of* Downbeat.

Dee

Ain't like him to stay away from the joint like this. Can't reach him at his apartment either.

Shanty

He don't come in but about once a day. Just to check things out—

Dee

It's a woman he's with, isn't it?

Shanty

Huh?

Dee

Hello?

Shanty

What you say? Eh, *que pasa?*

Dee

He's with a woman—it's a woman he's with . . .

Shanty

Uh—it's uh—Mel's day off, Dee—gotta go clean up the kitchen . . .

Dee

Shanty, come here a second . . .

> *He comes to her reluctantly.*

Thanks, huh?

> *She stuffs a bill into the pocket of his apron.*

For nothing!

> *He shrugs. Exits to kitchen. She goes back to drinking.*

Evie

> *Enters. Spies* DEE. *Moves to jukebox.*

Hey.

Dee

Hey, yourself!

> *Music comes on.*

How does it feel to be on your way to good citizenship?

Evie

Yeah, huh? Imagine me doin' it to an IBM machine.

81

Dee
It ain't hard.
Evie
That bottle ain't doin' you a damn bit'a good.

Dee
Tha's debatable.

Evie
How 'bout a nice hot cup'a black coffee?

Dee
Uh-uh! Gotta stay here an' wait for Johnny.

Evie
Pretty soon you'll be waitin' for him flat on the floor.

Dee
Drunk or sober, it doesn't matter anyway.

Evie
Why you doin' this? Sheee! He ain't worth the powder it'd take to
blow him up.

Dee
Tha's mah business.

Evie
It's my business you was up at Jack's last night.

Dee
Where'd you hear that?

Evie
Jack. He called me. Now, if you wanna kill yourself, or git killed—
go right ahead! But I wanna warn you 'bout one thing. Stay out'a
Jack's, you hear me? A lotta Niggers in there, jus' waitin' for somebody like you! 'Nother thing! Jack's my uncle—don't want'a see him
lose his license—on account'a some bitch like you!

Dee
Okay, so I was up at Jack's!

Evie
What was you lookin' for anyway? Way off yo' beat! Ain't nobody
up there got your price!

Dee
I wasn't sellin'—I was buyin'.

Evie
You was what?

Dee

The biggest blackest cat you ever saw picked me up.

Evie

You just lookin' to git yourself hurt, girl.

Dee

Oh, he was polite. Too polite. Took me to his room. Smelled like that greasy pomade an' hair straightener you smell sometimes on those pretties in the subway. An' when he put on his silk stocking-cap—I just about cracked. Kept the light on so he could watch.

Evie

Git yourself together, girl. Drunk as you are—you liable to tell Johnny 'bout this an' he'd have to kill you.

Dee

When it got good to him he started singin', "Black an' white together —black an' white together!" An' the toilet down the hall was flushing over and over again.

Evie

Bitch, did you hear what I said?

Dee

No! I ain't goin' anyplace! I'm stayin' right here . . .

> She sits at table. Goes into purse. Takes out can of shoe polish.

If I have to stage a sit-in to do it.

> She puts mirror before her. Begins to apply polish to her face.

Evie

Girl, what are you doin' . . .

Dee

> Knocks EVIE's hand away.

Take your hands off me, you stinkin' cunt! Dirty black sow!

Evie

> Slaps DEE viciously.

All right, you crazy, uptight, drunken whore! Sure as shit you gon' end up in Bellvue or git your ass sliced up an' thrown to the rats in some alley . . .

> JOHNNY enters. DEE sing-songs him.

Dee

Where you been keepin' yo'se'f, Johnneee, babeee!

Johnny

Git that crap off your face an' git the hell out'a here!

83

Dee

> *Snaps her fingers.*

I's black an' I's proud!

Evie

Listen here, Johnny! This girl is in trouble!

Johnny

She's free, white an' always right!

> DEE *laughs. He goes to her, wipes the black from her face, forcing her to relent.* DEE *begins to weep. He is almost tender with her.*

Evie

She ain't free a'you—Dee, if you got an ounce a sense left in yo' head you'll git on up and come on out with me now.

Dee

Hit the wind, sugar! Git on back to your stupid analyst an' your fuckin' IBM machine! Hit da win', sugar.

> EVIE *shakes her head, moves quickly to the door.*

Johnny

Hey! Pussy!

> *She turns angrily.*

I know what's eatin' yo' ass. You don't like it 'cause I went for her an' not you! Tha's it, ain't it?

Evie

> *Moves quickly to the two of them. Takes* DEE *by the shoulders. Pulls her up and draws her to her roughly. Plants a hard kiss upon* DEE's *mouth. She shoves* DEE *into the arms of* JOHNNY *who quickly puts* DEE *aside. He faces* EVIE *furiously.* SHANTY *enters.*

Darlin', you way off base. I've known Niggers like you all my life! Think everything's'a game. I wouldn't piss on you if yo' ass was on fire. Lef' to me, I'd give you a needle—let you sit in a corner like little Jackie Horner, jerkin' off all by yourself!

> JOHNNY *raises his hand.* EVIE *beats him to the punch, clubs him with her forefinger between the legs. He winces and doubles over.* EVIE *exits quickly.* DEE *laughs hysterically.* MARY LOU BOLTON *enters.* DEE *is lying on the floor.*

Mary Lou

Johnny, I . . .

Johnny

Stay where you at, Mary.

Mary Lou
Johnny, maybe I'd better . . .

Dee
Well, well, well. And just might who you be, Miss Baby Cakes?

Mary Lou
Johnny!

Johnny
I said stay where you at!

Dee
> *Struggles to her feet. Gathers her belongings.*

Baby Cakes, let me give you the best advice you ever had in your whole little life. Run away from here fast. Run for your life.
> *She goes into her purse. Comes up with baby shoes. Drops them on the floor. Exits.*

Mary Lou
Who is she, Johnny?

Johnny
Some chick with a problem.

Mary Lou
She—she looked . . .

Johnny
She was wiped out.

Mary Lou
> *Picks up the baby shoes.*

Who do these belong to . . .

Johnny
> *Snatches them out of her hands and throws them into the waste basket.*

Don't ask me! Never had no kid'a mine if tha's what you're thinkin'!

Mary Lou
I don't think you'll be seeing me anymore, Johnny.

Johnny
Why the hell not, Mary?

Mary Lou
Are you in any trouble, Johnny?

Johnny
Trouble? What kind'a trouble?

Mary Lou
85 My father! Someone called him about us!

Johnny
What about?

Mary Lou
Whoever it was said if he didn't stop me from seeing you, they would.
>   *He grins.*
Are you in some kind of trouble?

Johnny
That depen's, Mary. Take off, Shanty!

Shanty
Man, I still got . . .

Johnny
I said, take off!

>   SHANTY *takes off apron. Gets hat. Exits.* JOHNNY *locks doors behind him.*
'Member when we was talkin' 'bout Pete Zerroni?

Mary Lou
Yes . . .

Johnny
Pete don't like it if a Nigger's got a place'a business in his ter'tory.

Mary Lou
You gotta be kidding.

Johnny
Ain't you learned nothin' from all that civil rights?

Mary Lou
What proof do you have?

Johnny
Baby, this ain't no ord'nary type 'scrimunashun. They give you the signal. You ignore it. Place burns down.

Mary Lou
But why don't they want me to see you?

Johnny
Your ol' man was Zerroni's lawyer. Think maybe I might try to work you. . . .

Mary Lou
Work me?

Johnny
Yo' ol' man might have somethin' on Zerroni an' his boys in his records or files.

Mary Lou
That's silly! It could never be used as any real evidence.

86

Johnny

Sho' could make it hot for a whole lotta people if the D.A. happened to get a few tips.

Mary Lou

What are you getting at?

Johnny

Nothin'. You wanted to know why they didn't want you to see me, didn't you? 'Les yo' ol' man's prege'dice.

Mary Lou

He knows I've dated Negroes before.
> *She thinks for a moment.*
You really believe if you got this information it would keep Zerroni off your back?

Johnny

Well, they still don't know who killed Rep'senative Mahoney. . . .

Mary Lou

Well, you know I couldn't do anything like that. I mean take that information. My father would never forgive me.

Johnny

Like I say. Tha's the only reason I kin figger why they don't want you to be seein' me.

Mary Lou

Anyway, he keeps that sort of thing locked in a safe! In his office.

Johnny

> *Comes to her. Takes her by the hand and pulls her to him.*
> *He kisses her gently. She responds.*
Queer, ain't it? Yo' ol' man's a judge. Sworn to uphol' justice. We cain't even go to him for help.

Mary Lou

I'll speak to him about it, Johnny.

Johnny

Don't you do that, Mary. Don't you do nothin' like that.

Mary Lou

But why, Johnny? He could probably help you.

Johnny

For all we know, he might be in with Zerroni.

Mary Lou

Don't you say that.

Johnny

Funny, after that rotten bunch'a Ginees got off he got to be judge right away.

Mary Lou

I think I'd better leave now.

Johnny

Why'd you come back here, Mary? Make like you wanted a daiquiri. Think I'd be a sucker for some white missionary pussy?

Mary Lou

That is a terrible thing to say.

Johnny

You don't give a dam about civil rights. What about my civil rights? Don't I git any?

Mary Lou

There are ways to stop Zerroni. There are people we can go to for help.

Johnny

Yeah? An' they'll go over to Zerroni's an' picket!

Mary Lou

That's not funny.

Johnny

You liberal-ass white people kill me! All the time know more 'bout wha's bes' for Niggers'n Niggers do.

Mary Lou

You don't have to make the world any worse.

Johnny

Never had no chance to make it no better neither.

> There is pounding on street doors. JOHNNY unlocks them.
> MARY LOU rushes out as GABE hurries in.

Gabe

Git your coat, John. Quick!

Johnny

What the hell for?

Gabe

It's Dee! She's dead.

Johnny

Dead?

Gabe

Can't figger how they got my number. She slit her wrists. Why'd they call me?

Johnny
Where is she?

Gabe
The ladies' room. Hotel Theresa.
Blackout.

SCENE TWO

Time: Three days later
Place: The same
Setting: The same
At rise: Music from jukebox is going full blast. SHANTY is seated on a barstool. Beats on the next stool with drumsticks.

Shanty
Aw, blow it, baby! Workout! Yeah! I hear ya! Swing it! Work yo' show!

> *JOHNNY and GABE enter dressed in suits. GABE as usual carries briefcase.*

Johnny
Goddamit, Shanty! Git under the bed with that shit. Ain't you got no respect for the dead?

> *Pulls cord out of socket. SHANTY puts sticks away. MELVIN comes out of kitchen.*

Melvin
How was the funeral?

Gabe
How is any funeral, Mel?

Johnny

> *Goes behind bar. Mixes drinks.*

Every damned whore in town showed up! Think they'd have a little respeck an' stay home!

Melvin
Was her people there?

Gabe
Only us!

Shanty
> *Picks up newspaper.*
Paper sure gave you hell, Johnny!

Johnny
Who the hell asked ya?
> *He comes around bar.*
Comin' on like some bitch in'a cheap-ass movie! Writin' all that jive on the shithouse wall with lipstick!

Shanty
I always liked Dee! Good tipper.

Johnny
> *Bangs on bar.*
Anybody'd think I killed her! Blamin' me for everything! Hell, I never did nothin' to her!

Gabe
Nothin' for her neither!

Cora
> *Enters. Dressed to kill. Wears white rose corsage.*
Hello, ev'body.

Gabe
Hello, Cora. . . .

Cora
Wha's ev'body lookin' so down in the mouth about? Like you jus' come from a funeral.

Johnny
Is that yo' idea of some kind'a damn joke?

Melvin
Ain't you heard, Cora?

Cora
Heard what?

Melvin
It's been in all the papers! Johnny's friend, Dee. She committed suicide a couple of days ago.

Cora
Lawd have mercy! I'm so sorry! I—I haven't exactly been keepin' up with the news lately! You see I—I jus' got married this morning.

92

Melvin

Married? I hope you'll be very happy, Cora.

Gabe

Congratulations, Cora.

Cora

Oh, thank you! Thank you so much.

Johnny

Must'a been a whirlwin' co'tship.

Cora

Ack-shully, I been knowin' him f'quite some time! He's a heart spesh-lis' I met at the hospital.

Johnny

From the looks of you, he mus' be a pretty good'n.

Cora

He's jus' aroun' the corner gittin' the car checked over! It's a good distance to Kwee-beck.

Gabe

Quebec?

Cora

Our honeymoon! Wants me to meet his peoples! 'Cause they's French, you know. Jay Cee?

> *She goes to* JOHNNY.

Johnny

What?

Cora

Awful sorry 'bout what happened.

Johnny

Yeah! Sure, Cora!

Cora

Sump'm ter'ble must'a happen to drive her to do a thing like that!

Johnny

Good luck with the married bag, huh?

Cora

Why, thank you, Jay Cee! Thank you. You know me an' you knowed each other a lotta years. Some reason, I could never do nothin' to suit you. No matter how hard I tried. Sometimes you make me so mad I ha'f wanna kill you! But I was fool 'nuff to care sump'm 'bout you anyway. 'Cause to me you always been that li'l bad boy who was lef' all alone in the worl' with nobody to take care him!

93

Johnny

Guess it'll always be "Jay Cee ag'inst the worl'!"

Cora

> *Tries to touch him. He jerks away. She looks at* SHANTY.

Ain't you gon' wish me good luck too, Shangy Mulligans?

> SHANTY *remains silent. Stares out of the window. She shrugs. Moves to street doors.*

Well, o-re-vo-ree, ev'body! O-re-vo-ree!

> *She giggles.*

Tha's French, you know! That means, "Bye, y'all!"

> *She exits happily.*

Shanty

Se-la-goddam-vee.

Melvin

She sure was happy!

Gabe

Different too.

Johnny

Married a doctor! Ain't that a bitch? Say one thing for her! That number don't give up! She . . .

Shanty

Shut up, man!

Johnny

What you say?

Shanty

I said shut up, nigger.

Johnny

Now, look. I know you upset 'bout Cora, but . . .

Shanty

Will you cool it! Big man! Mister hot daddy! Think you know everything in the whole goddam world, don't you? Well, lemme tell you somethin', man. You don't know a mu-thah-fuc-kun thing.

> *He rips off his apron and flings it into* JOHNNY's *face.*

Here! Do your own dirty Nigger work! I've done all I'm gonna do! Took all I'm gonna take!

> *He pulls out his drumsticks. Boldly beats on the bar*

Stood behind this bar! Let you put me down for the last time 'cause my skin is white.

> *He beats harder on the bar.*

Yeah, baby. I'm white. An' I'm proud of it. Pretty an' white. Dynamite.   94

Eh, mothah fuckah. Know what else I got that you ain't got? I got soul. You ain't got no soul. Mothahfuckah's black an' ain't got no soul. If you're an example of what the white race is ag'inst, then baby, I'm gittin' with 'em. They are gonna need a cat like me. Somebody that really knows where you black sons-a-bitches are at.

> *He picks up the butcher knife. Plunges it into the top of the bar.*

That's what I think of this ol' piece'a kindlin'! Take it an' stick it up you black, rusty, dusty!

> *He moves quickly to the street doors. Turns. Gives JOHNNY the finger and exits quickly.*

Johnny
Well, looks like ol' Corabelle Beasely done turned Shanty into a real white man, after all. Now, what about you, Mel?

Melvin
Huh?

Johnny
Don't you wanna cuss me out an' split too?

Melvin
I ain't got nothin' against you, Johnny.

Johnny
Tha's too damn bad.

> *Tosses Melvin some bills.*

Melvin
What's this for, Johnny?

Johnny
Cain't afford to keep the kitchen open no more. Business all aroun' ain't worth lickin' the lead on a pencil.

Melvin
Let me stay on, Johnny, please? Shanty's gone. I can tend bar and still do whatever short orders there are. Please, Johnny, don't let me go.

Johnny
Dam, Mel. Didn't know you liked it aroun' here that much.

Gabe
What about your dancin', Mel? You wanna work in a bar the rest of your life?

Melvin
I—I quit my dancin', Gabe. . . .

Gabe
95 Why'd you do that?

Melvin

Well, I—I went to this party Victor gave at his penthouse. A lot of celebrities were there. And Gabe, you just wouldn't have believed it.

Gabe

What happened?

Melvin

I'm ashamed to tell you!

Johnny

Aw, go on, Mel. We big boys.

Melvin

Well, they all got plastered! They were smoking marihuana, too! Even the women! Can you imagine? And then they started taking off their clothes.

Johnny

Didn't you know where these turkeys was at before you went?

Melvin

I don't go to parties much. I don't drink. You know that.

Johnny

Did you take your clothes off too?

Melvin

Are you kidding?

Gabe

So you left.

Melvin

They wouldn't let me leave. So I ran into that bathroom and locked that door. But they jimmied the door open.

Johnny

An' then what happened?

Melvin

They—they held me down and took all my clothes off. It was awful. I said if that's what you gotta do to be a dancer then . . .

Johnny

Mel, yo' mama must'a gave you too many hot baths when you was a baby.

Mary Lou

> Enters. She carries a paper bag.

Helped my father at the office yesterday. Must have watched him dial the combination to that safe at least twenty times.

> JOHNNY snatches bag. Locks doors. Comes behind bar.
> MARY LOU follows.

96

Didn't get a chance to hear the tapes. Glanced through some of the other stuff, though. Looks pretty explosive.

Johnny
Don't read so good, Mary. What's this stuff say?

Mary Lou
Zerroni admits that he had Joseph Mahoney killed! Maffucci did it. And here it says that he was in on several bribes . . .

Johnny
Mary, this is it. This is the stuff I need!

Mary Lou
I—I thought about it a long time. There just wasn't any other solution.
                    JOHNNY *stuffs papers back into bag.*
Johnny, I—I . . .
                    She peers at GABE *and* MELVIN.

Johnny
Go 'head! You kin say anything in front'a them.

Mary Lou
Well, it's not the kind of thing you would say in front of . . .

Johnny
Mary, I don't think it's wise for you to be seen aroun' here. I want you to lay low for a while.

Mary Lou
I can't go home, Johnny. Daddy will know I . . .

Johnny
Ain't they some girlfri'n you kin stay with?

Mary Lou
I—I suppose so. But I thought we . . .

Gabe
What's this all about, John?

Mary Lou
It's to keep Pete Zerroni from forcing Johnny out of business. Don't you know about it?

Melvin
First time I've heard about it.

Gabe
What's your father got to do with it?

Mary Lou
97   He was Zerroni's lawyer.

Gabe

And you stole that material from your father?

Mary Lou

Yes, I stole that material from my father. There was nothing else we could do.

Gabe

Why, you stupid, naive little bitch. Don't you know what he wants that stuff for?

Mary Lou

To keep Zerroni from forcing him out of business.

Gabe

That's a lie! He wants it so he kin blackmail his way into his own dirty racket.

Mary Lou

That's not true! Tell him, Johnny.

Gabe

A black Mafia. That's what he wants.

> GABE *laughs.*

Mary Lou

You're crazy. Johnny, are you going to stand there and . . .

Johnny

I gotta right to my own game. Just like they do.

Mary Lou

What?

Johnny

My own game!

Mary Lou

Johnny!

Gabe

What did you do it for, Mary? For love? Sheee! He hates you, you bitch. Hates everything you stand for. Nice little suffering white girl.

> MARY LOU *slaps* GABE. *He throws her into a chair. She begins to weep.*

Lemme tell you something. Before he kin lay one hot hand on you, you gonna have to git out there on that street an' hussle your ass off.

> GABE *moves to* JOHNNY.

Gimme that file, John.

> JOHNNY *reaches under bar. Comes up with revolver. Levels it at* GABE. MELVIN *gasps. Falls to floor.*

Johnny
I don't wanna kill you, Gabe. This is the one break I been waitin' on.
It ain't much but it's gon' have to do.

Gabe
You kill me that file ain't gonna do you no good anyway. I'm tellin'
you. Gimme that file.

> JOHNNY *finally lowers gun.* GABE *puts bag into briefcase.*
> *Starts to move to street doors.* MAFFUCCI *and* JUDGE BOL-
> TON *enter.*

Bolton
Get in the car, Mary Lou.

Mary Lou
Daddy, I . . .

Bolton
I said get in the car!

> MARY LOU *rushes out, followed by* MAFFUCCI.

You know what I'm here for, Williams.

Johnny
Just like that, huh?

Bolton
Just like that.

> MAFFUCCI *reenters.*

Johnny
I wanna talk to Pete Zerroni.

Maffucci
Pete ain't got nothin' to say to you, Johnny Cake.

Bolton
Those notes belong to me. Not to Zerroni.

Johnny
I ain't budgin' till I see Pete, personal. He's got to come here an' go
horse-to-horse with me. Ain't gon' wait too long neither. 'Lection's
comin' up. Li'l phone call to the D.A. could make him very happy
'bout his future.

> MAFFUCCI *suddenly pulls gun on* JOHNNY.

Bolton
Put that away, you fool!

> MAFFUCCI *returns gun to shoulder holster.*

Johnny
Footch, don't think Pete or the Judge here wanna see me git hit jus'
yet.

Bolton
What is it, Williams? Money?
> *Produces an envelope.*

Johnny
You ofays sho' think money's the root'a all evil, don't you, judge?

Maffucci
Let's go, Frank. We're just wastin' time.

Bolton
Williams, you'd better listen to me and listen good. You're in dangerous trouble. If you don't hand over that material, I'm not going to be responsible for what happens to you.

Johnny
An' I sho' ain't gon' be responsible for what happens to you neither, Judge.
> *Both* JOHNNY *and the* JUDGE *laugh.* BOLTON *starts to exit.*

Judge?
> BOLTON *turns.* JOHNNY *tosses him* MARY LOU's *purse.* BOLTON *exits.*

Maffucci
Johnny Cake?

Johnny
What?

Maffucci
Right now, your life ain't worth a plug nickel.

Johnny
Footch?
> *Puts his thumbnail under his upper teeth and flicks it at* MAFFUCCI. MAFFUCCI *exits.*

Johnny
Gabe-ree-el. How come you didn't hand over the file?

Gabe
I couldn't! When I saw those two bastards together, I just couldn't bring myself to do it!
> GABE *removes bag from briefcase. Hands it to* JOHNNY.

Johnny
Mel, take this over to the drugstore. Get copies made, quick! Move!
> MELVIN *exits quickly.*

Gabe
You know they're gonna git you.

Johnny
Gabe, we was got the day we was born! Where you been? Jus' bein'
black ain't never been no real reason for livin'.

Gabe
If I thought that I'd probably go crazy or commit suicide.
Blackout.

SCENE THREE

Time: A day later
Place: The same
Setting: The same
At rise: JOHNNY is seated on a barstool, checking his gun. GABE exits to kitchen. MACHINE DOG appears wearing a shabby military uniform.

Machine Dog
I don't work at the garage no more, brother.

Johnny
You jive. You don't know nothin' else.

Machine Dog
They's other work to be done. They's other mo' important things to be worked on and fixed. Like my black brothers. They needs fixin' bad. Tha's when I got to thinkin'a you, Brother Williams.

Johnny
Yea, well you can just kick them farts at somebody else.

Machine Dog
On yo' feet, mothah fuckah!

> *JOHNNY comes to his feet militarily. MACHINE DOG presents a Nazi-like salute.*

By the powers invested in me by the brothers I hereby deliver to you the edick!

> *JOHNNY and MACHINE DOG give each other some skin.*
> *MACHINE DOG goes back to his salute.*

Brother Williams. The brothers have jus' sennunced an' condemned you to death. Now, repeat after me. I have been chosen to be the nex' brother to live on in the hearts an' min's'a the enemy host.

Johnny
I have been chosen to be the nex' brother to live on in the hearts an' min's'a the enemy host.

Machine Dog
My duty will be to ha'nt they cripple an' sore min's.

Johnny
My duty will be to haunt they cripple an' sore min's.

Machine Dog
I will cling to the innermos' closets'a they brains an' agonize them.

Johnny
I will cling to the innermos' closets'a they brains an' agonize them.

Machine Dog
> Breaks *his salute and gives an aside.*
Maniacks though they is already!
> *He goes back into his salute.*
The more they will try to cas' me out, the mo' they torment will be.

Johnny
The more they will try to cast me out, the more they torment will be!

Machine Dog
Se la an' ayman!
> MACHINE DOG *shakes* JOHNNY's *hand.*
You will have plen'y'a he'p, Brother Williams. All them brothers that went before you an' all them tha's comin' after you.

Johnny
I gladly accept the condemnashun, Gen'ral Sheen. Tell the brothers I won't let 'em down. Tell 'em I look forward to meetin' 'em all in par'dise.

Machine Dog
Se la! An' ayman!
> *They salute each other.*

Johnny
Se la an' ay-man!
> MACHINE DOG *goes into kitchen as* JUDGE BOLTON *and two plainclothesmen,* CAPPALETTI *and* HARRY, *enter.*

Bolton
This is the man, Al!
> CAPPALETTI *flashes his badge.*

Cappaletti
Cappaletti. Vice squad.

Johnny
Big deal!

Cappaletti
Judge Bolton, here. His daughter was picked up this afternoon.

Johnny
So what?

Cappaletti
She tried to solicit this officer here.

Johnny
What's that got to do with me?

Cappaletti
Said she was workin' for you.

Johnny
Tha's a lie. Tha's a goddam lie. Lemme hear say that to my face.

Cappaletti
Plenty of time for that.

Johnny
What the hell you tryin' to pull, Bolton?

Cappaletti
Now, why would the Judge wanna pull anything on you, Johnny?

Johnny
He—he don't want his daughter seein' me. 'Cause I'm a Nigger. I'll lay odds she don't know nothin' about this.

Cappaletti
Go get Miss Bolton, Harry.
          HARRY moves to street doors.

Johnny
Hurry, Harry!
          HARRY grins. Exits.

Cappaletti
By the way. Ain't you the guy this girl killed herself about a few days ago? She was a call girl?

Johnny
Tell you like I tole them other fuzzys. What she did was her own business.

Cappaletti
Just the same you kin see how we kin believe Miss Bolton's story.

HARRY *leads* MARY LOU *into bar.* CAPPALETTI *seats her.*
Now, Miss Bolton. We'll ask you again. Who did you say you was workin' for when you was picked up?

Mary Lou
I—I . . .

Cappaletti
Speak up, Miss Bolton. We can't hear you.

Mary Lou
Daddy, I . . .

Bolton
All you have to do is identify him. Is he the man?
CAPPALETTI *puts his hand on* MARY LOU's *head.*
Take your hands off her!
HARRY *laughs.*
Mary Lou! Is he or isn't he?

Mary Lou
Forces herself to face JOHNNY.
Yes! This is the man! Johnny Williams! I was working for him!
MARY LOU *rushes from bar followed by* HARRY.

Johnny
Dirty lyin' bitch.

Bolton
Now, see here, Williams!

Cappaletti
You're gonna have to come with me, Johnny.

Johnny
What is this, a pinch? You gonna book me? I'm gonna call my lawyer!

Cappaletti
Shut up! You're not callin' nobody right now. Let's go.

Bolton
Just a minute, Al. I want a few words with him before you take him down.

Cappaletti
Okay, Frank, but make it snappy.

Bolton
Williams, I've worked too long and too hard to get where I am. I'm giving you one last chance to give back those notes and tape. If you don't, it's on the bottom of the woodpile for you. Even if I have to sacrifice my own daughter to do it. I want that file.

Johnny
Okay, Judge. Okay. You win.

> JOHNNY *goes behind bar. Brings out paper bag.* JUDGE *checks it. Nods to* CAPPALETTI *and exits.*

Cappaletti
All right, Johnny. All of a sudden the Judge wants me to forget the whole thing. Lucky we didn't get you down to the precinct. Would have busted you up on general principles.

> CAPPALETTI *exits. Quickly* JOHNNY *puts his revolver into his back pocket. Goes behind the bar.*

Johnny
Better split, Gabe. While the gittin's good.

Gabe
Don't think so, John. I'm gonna stick aroun'.

Johnny
Suit yo'self!

> *Doors open.* JOHNNY *goes for his gun.* SWEETS CRANE *enters. He is practically in tatters. He carries a shopping bag. Goes to table and begins to take out various articles of food. He coughs and rubs his hands together.*

Sweets
I got fried chicken! Ham! Candied yams! Got me some hot chit'lin's! Blackeyed peas an' rice! Cornbread! Mustard greens an' macaroni salit!

> *Coughs.*

Top ev'thing off I got me'a thermos full'a—full'a—lemme see now. How'd my gran'daddy used to call it? Chassy San'burg coffee!

> *Laughs.*

An' a big chunk'a pee-kan pie. Y'all fellas is welcomed to join me.

Johnny
Wouldn't touch it if it was blessed by the pope!

Sweets
Well, now tha's a dam shame. 'Member when I couldn't pull you away from my cookin'.

Gabe
You don't mind if I join him, do you, John?

Johnny
Be my guest.

Sweets
He'p yo'se'f, young fella. They's plen'y here. Have some'a these here chit'lin's!

Gabe

Ain't never had none before.

Sweets

Then let this be the day you start.

> GABE *takes a sniff.*

Go 'head! Go 'head! You don't eat the smell.

Gabe

Lemme ask you sump'm, Sweets.

Sweets

Hope I kin answer it.

Gabe

How come you took my watch an' wallet?

Sweets

Son, all my life I been one kind'a thief or 'nother. It's jus' in me. 'Course I don't have to steal. But I steals for the pure enjoyment of it. Jus' the other day I stole a rat'la from a baby.

> *Laughs.*

When you steals for fun it don't matter who you steals from!

> *Goes into his pocket. Comes up with* GABE's *watch and wallet.*

Gabe

It's all here!

Sweets

'Co'se it is! Gave the baby back his rat'la too.

Johnny

You ain't gon' make the white man's heaven this way.

Sweets

The Lawd died 'tween two thieves.

Maffucci

> *Enters with* LOUIE.

Wouldn't listen to me, would you, Johnny Cake?

Johnny

What Pete say? Give a jig a half'a chance . . .

Sweets

This the fella work for big fat Pete, Sonny Boy?

Maffucci

What's it to ya, Pops? You an' this other joker better get the hell out'a here before you catch cold.

Sweets

I ain't never got up from a meal in my life 'fore I was finished . . .   108

Maffucci

Look, Pops! Don't make me have to . . .
> *Glances at food.*

What's that? Macaroni salad you got there?

Sweets

Matter fack it is!

Maffucci
> *Dips into it.*

Ummm! Not bad. Who made it?

Sweets

I did.

Maffucci

No kiddin'? Knew it didn't taste like dela-ga-tes. Mama used to make macaroni salad.

Sweets

Have'a piece'a my fried chicken to go with it.

Johnny

If Zerroni could see you now, Footch.

Maffucci

How's that, Johnny Cake?

Johnny

Tha's the great Sweets Crane you eatin' with.

Maffucci

Pops, here? He's Sweets Crane?

Sweets

What's lef' of me.

Maffucci

You'd'a made out better as a cook, Pops. Mama couldn't beat that macaroni salad!

Sweets
> *Produces MAFFUCCI's watch.*

I think this b'longs to you.

Maffucci

My watch! I been lookin' all over for it. Pops, you copped my watch?
> *Laughs.*

How come you're givin' it back? This watch is worth a lotta bread.

Sweets

Figger you need it wors'n I do.

Maffucci

Say, Johnny Cake, you sure Pops here is Sweets Crane?

Johnny

You don't know how much I wish he wasn't.

Maffucci

Too bad Johnny didn't learn a lesson after what happened to you, Pops. Gotta give him credit though. Takes a lotta balls to try to put the bleed on Pete Zerroni.

Sweets

You was tryin' to blackmail ol' big fat Pete, Sonny Boy?

Johnny

What the hell. Couldn't pull it off. Don't matter much now.

Maffucci

That's where you're wrong, Johnny Cake. Matters a helluva lot to me. Pete now, he's willin' to forget the whole thing. Says the trick is not to take you jigs too serious. I can't do nothin' like that, Johnny. Don't look good on my record.

Johnny

What you gonna do about it, Footch?

> MAFFUCCI *quickly pulls his gun. Levels it at* JOHNNY. *Backs to street doors. Locks them. Pulls shades. Takes a large sign from his pocket. It reads, "CLOSED." He puts it on the bar in front of* JOHNNY.

The sign in both hands, Johnny Cake.

> JOHNNY *slowly picks up sign.*

Pops, you an' that other joker stay put!

> MAFFUCCI *nods to* LOUIE *who moves behind* SWEETS *and* GABE. JOHNNY *starts to tear sign.*

Ah-ah! I want you to lick that sign an' paste it right up there on the door. Start lickin', Johnny Cake!

> JOHNNY *begins to wet sign with his tongue.*

That's it! Wet it up a little more! That's enough! Now start walkin' real careful like!

> JOHNNY *moves to street door with sign.*

Now, paste it up there!

> *Johnny does so.*

Now, back up! Real slow!

> JOHNNY *backs up.* MAFFUCCI *seats* JOHNNY *on a barstool.*

Sweets

You don't have to do that, Sonny Boy.

> *Goes to the door with knife he has been eating with.*

You don't have to do nothin' like that.

> *He pulls the sign from the window and tears it up.*

110

Maffucci

What are you doin', Pops? Look, if you don't want hi-call-it to get hit ...

Johnny

Keep out'a this, Sweets. This is my game.

Sweets

Not any more, it ain't. You don't have to do nothin' like that.

> *Advances to MAFFUCCI.*

Maffucci

What'a ya, crazy, Pops? Put that ax away.

Johnny

Lay out of it, Sweets. Lay out of it, I said!

Maffucci

I'm warnin' you, Pops! Take another step an' ...

> SWEETS *lunges at MAFFUCCI as MAFFUCCI fires. Knife penetrates MAFFUCCI's heart. JOHNNY kills LOUIE. Whirls and fires three shots into MAFFUCCI. Rushes to SWEETS.*

Johnny

Goddamit, Sweets! I tole you I could handle it!

Gabe

I'll call a doctor!

Sweets

Fuck a doctor! Cain't you see I'm dead?

> *Coughs. Winces in pain.*

Lissen to me, Sonny Boy! You—you gotta promise me one thing ...

Johnny

What is it, Sweets?

Sweets

The—the will! It's here in—in my pocket.

> JOHNNY *finds will.*

If—if you git out'a this. Promise you'll git straightened out.

> *He grabs JOHNNY's arm.*

Promise!

Johnny

I—I promise.

Sweets

Swear!

Johnny

Yeah! Yeah! I swear, Sweets!

Sweets
Git—git rid'a the—the Ch-Cholly fever—
>SWEETS *goes limp.*

Gabe
He did it for you, John . . .

Johnny
Look, Gabe. We gotta git our story together. When the fuzz gits here we gotta have us a story.

Gabe
We tell 'em the truth, John . . .

Johnny
What you say?

Gabe
We tell the police the truth!

Johnny
Shit. The truth is I'm alive! I got a copy'a that file an' Sweets' will.

Gabe
But you tole Sweets you was gonna throw them ideas out'a your head.

Johnny
Come on, man, you didn't think I meant that shit, did you?

Gabe
With his last dyin' breath, you gave that ol' man your word. You swore.

Johnny
What good is anybody's word to that ol' bastard? He's dead an' cain't remember.

Gabe
You are mad.

Johnny
I'm goin' ahead with my plans.
>*He holds up will.*

An' he's still gon' help me do it.

Gabe
Naw, naw! That ain't the way it's s'pose to be!

Johnny
You in this as deep as I am. It's our word ag'inst these dead turkeys. You gave me back that file, remember?

Gabe
That's where I got off. I ain't got no stomach for this personal war you got ag'inst the white man.

112

Johnny

It's your war too, Nigger. Why can't you see that? You wanna go on believin' in the lie? We at war, Gabe! Black ag'inst white.

Gabe

You're wrong, John. You're so goddam wrong.

> JOHNNY *picks up gun. Puts it into* GABE's *hand.*

Johnny

Take this gun in yo' han'. Feel that col' hard steel. Bet you ain't never held a heater in yo' han' like that in yo' life. Well, you gon' have to, Gabe. They gon' make you do it. 'Cause we at war, Gabe. Black ag'inst white.

Gabe

I—I don't wanna—kill—you . . .

Johnny

You ain't got the guts! You wanna believe you kin sell papers an' be-come President! You're a coward, Gabe! A lousy, yellow, screamin' faggot coward!

> Enraged, GABE *fires at* JOHNNY. JOHNNY *tumbles back-ward and then forward into* GABE's *arms.* GABE *eases* JOHNNY *to the floor.* JOHNNY *goes limp.* MACHINE DOG *enters.*

Gabe

> *Startled.*

Who're you? Where did you come from?

Machine Dog

The Brothers call me Machine Dog! It is written: "He that slays a true brother, he hisse'f shall howsomever be perished!"

Gabe

He made me kill him! He . . .

> During MACHINE DOG's *speech,* GABE *takes gun. Wipes it off. Places it in* JOHNNY's *hand. Covers* JOHNNY *with tablecloth. Exits.*

Machine Dog

Hush yo' lyin', trait-ious tongue! Ver'ly, ver'ly, I says into you! You has kilt all them li'l innusunt cherbs'a the ghetto! Them li'l rams who been hatin' 'thorty eb'm from the cradle! All them holy de-lin-cunts who been the true creators'a unsolved thef's an' killin's! You has slewn an' slaughtered them young goateed billygoats who been dedcated to that sanctified an' precious art'a lootin' the destruction'a private pub-lic poverty! You has hung an' lynched the black angels'a color who went by that high code'a rooftops an' been baptized in the stink of urine scented hallways! You has burnt an' melted down a million switchblade knives an' razors an' broke preshus bottles'a communion upon the empty white-paved streets'a the enemy host! An' lef' the brothers thirsty an' col' to bang the doors'a the guilty white Samaritan! You has crushed the very life fum black an' profane souls! Hordes'a un-re-gen-rants! An' smashed the spirit an' holy ghost fum rollers an' dancers who founded they faith on black, human sufferin'! Burnt an' tortured souls who knew th'ough the power of love that they trials an' trib'lashuns could not be leg'slated away by no co't, no congruss, not eb'm God Hisse'f! You has scortched an' scalded them black Mo-heekans an' stuffed them in the very stoves they cooked on! Se la! An' ay-man!

 Blackout.

EPILOGUE

GABE *enters dressed as a woman in mourning. A black
shawl is draped over his head.*

Gabe

Like my costume? You like it? You don't like it! I know what I am by
what I see in your faces. You are my mirrors. But unlike a metallic re-
flection, you will not hold my image for very long. Your capacity for
attention is very short. Therefore, I must try to provoke you. Provoke
your attention. Change my part over and over again. I am rehears-
ing at the moment. For tomorrow, I will go out amongst you, "The
Black Lady in Mourning." I will weep, I will wail, and I will mourn. But
my cries will not be heard. No one will wipe away my bitter tears. My
black anguish will fall upon deaf ears. I will mourn a passing! Yes.
The passing and the ending of a people dying. Of a people dying into
that new life. A people whose identity could only be measured by the
struggle, the dehumanization, the degradation they suffered. Or al-
lowed themselves to suffer perhaps. I will mourn the ending of those
years. I will mourn the death of a people dying. Of a people dying into
that new life.

     Blackout.

THE END